5

THINGS

EVERY
CHRISTIAN
NEEDS TO
GROW

R. C. SPROUL

 LIGONIER MINISTRIES

Five Things Every Christian Needs to Grow
© 2008 by R.C. Sproul

Published by Ligonier Ministries
421 Ligonier Court, Sanford, FL 32771
Ligonier.org

Printed in Ann Arbor, Michigan
Cushing-Malloy, Inc.
0000122
Second edition, third paperback printing

ISBN 978-1-64289-259-8 (Paperback)
ISBN 978-1-56769-103-0 (Hardcover)
ISBN 978-1-56769-239-6 (ePub)
ISBN 978-1-56769-761-2 (Kindle)

Cover design: José Reyes for Metaleap Design
Interior design and typeset: Katherine Lloyd, The DESK

Scripture taken from the New King James Version ®. Copyright © 1982 by Thomas Nelson. Used by permission. All rights reserved.

Library of Congress has cataloged the Reformation Trust edition as follows:

Sproul, R.C. (Robert Charles), 1939-2017
 Five things every Christian needs to grow / R.C. Sproul. -- 2nd ed.
    p. cm.
 ISBN 978-1-56769-103-0
 1. Christian life--Reformed authors. I. Title.
 BV4501.3.S665 2008
 248.4--dc22

                                                    2008020821

To Archie Parrish,
for his utter devotion to kingdom-focused prayer,

and to Douglas M. Rhoda,
for his zeal to see this book made available again,
that Christians might be aided in their spiritual growth.

Contents

Introduction

It's a worldwide phenomenon. Every four years, the world pauses and holds its collective breath while the Olympic Games take place. Staggered so they occur two years apart, the summer and winter games feature the finest athletes in the world competing in well-known sports such as running, skiing, basketball, and gymnastics, as well as comparatively unknown events such as curling and the triple jump. The athletes come from virtually every nation on the face of the earth, a vast, magnificent display of humanity in all its diversity: different skin colors, different languages, different dress styles, and different lifestyles.

But despite their differences, these national representatives have much in common as they enter the stadium and gather under the Olympic banner with its five interlocking rings representing unity among the nations of Africa, the Americas, Asia, Australia, and Europe. They all stand together and take the Olympic oath, pledging to uphold the highest ideals of sportsmanship. They all strive to attain the Olympic ideal: *Citius, Altius, Fortius* (Swifter, Higher, Stronger). And they all put their years of training and preparation to the utmost test, going head to head against their fellow competitors.

Being a Christian is not an acquired skill or discipline like diving or ice skating. It is a living, vital relationship with the God of the universe, a relationship that begins when a person becomes a new creation in Him and receives Jesus as Lord by faith. But like Olympic athletes, Christians are called upon to train, to make sacrifices, and to embrace certain disciplines in order to give God "our utmost for His highest." This book deals with five of those disciplines: Bible study, prayer, worship, service, and stewardship. Just as Olympic athletes work hard to achieve their best performances, our diligence in attending to these aspects of the Christian life will help determine our effectiveness in serving our Lord.

Olympians sweat and sacrifice for years and sometimes decades for the chance to compete and, hopefully, win a medal and hear the applause of fans the world over. This stands as a once-in-a-lifetime experience for a select few gifted and dedicated men and women. God's people likely will not receive the world's adulation, but we will someday hear the words, "Well done, good and faithful servant."

> Do you not know that those who run in a race all run, but one receives the prize? Run in such a way that you may obtain it. And everyone who competes for the prize is temperate in all things. Now they do it to obtain a perishable crown, but we for an imperishable crown. (1 Cor. 9:24–25)

Enjoy your race.

Chapter 1

BIBLE STUDY

The man writhed in excruciating agony. The pain he felt was not physical. He wished it were; he had dealt with that kind of pain before, and he knew he could find relief from it. But this pain required something much greater for its cure. This was a spiritual agony, a darkness of the soul in which he felt suspended by a fragile filament over the gaping jaws of hell. The pain was the shame, devastation, and ruin of personal humiliation brought on by the public exposure of a secret sin.

This man had been a hero, a national celebrity, a noted warrior, statesman, poet, and musician. During his lifetime, he had been the object of popular songs that celebrated his exploits. He had catapulted to national fame when he had championed his people by killing his army's most feared enemy, a monstrous titan, simply with a sling and one smooth stone. He had been a loyal subject of his king, even when that man had sought to kill him. Later, he had become king himself, and his reign had ushered in the golden age of Israel as he extended the boundaries of the nation to unprecedented lengths. Situated on the land bridge that connects Africa with Asia and Europe, through which ran international trade routes, Israel was positioned in a place of strategic geopolitical importance. Under this man's leadership, this tiny country, about the size of the state of Maryland, had become a major world power. But his greatness went beyond politics and culture. He had been a spiritual leader, a man after God's own heart. He was David, the second king of Israel.

When he fell into monstrous sin, it was a calamity not only for David and his family, but also for the entire nation. Despite his spiritual strength, he was so blinded to the evil in his own heart that it took a direct confrontation by the prophet Nathan to awaken David to his guilt. We read the account in 2 Samuel 12:1–7:

> Then the LORD sent Nathan to David. And he came to him, and said to him:
>
> "There were two men in one city, one rich and the other poor. The rich man had exceedingly many flocks and herds. But the poor man had nothing, except one little ewe lamb which he had bought and nourished; and it grew up together with him and with his children. It ate of his own food and drank from his own cup and lay in his bosom; and it was like a daughter to him. And a traveler came to the rich man, who refused to take from his own flock and from his own herd to prepare one for the wayfaring man who had come to him; but he took the poor man's lamb and prepared it for the man who had come to him."
>
> So David's anger was greatly aroused against the man, and he said to Nathan, "As the LORD lives, the man who has done this shall surely die! And he shall restore fourfold for the lamb, because he did this thing and because he had no pity."
>
> Then Nathan said to David, "You are the man!"

David was grief-stricken at this unmasking, this indictment. Verse 13 says, "So David said to Nathan, 'I have sinned against the LORD.'" Through Nathan's words, David was stricken by the convicting power of the Holy Spirit. His repentance was as deep as his fall had been steep. His remorse went beyond a superficial fear of punishment to authentic repentance, a spirit marked by a heart broken for offending God.

In this attitude of contrition, David penned the prayer known to us as Psalm 51. In this psalm, all the elements of true repentance are found:

Have mercy upon me, O God,
According to Your lovingkindness;
According to the multitude of Your tender mercies,
Blot out my transgressions.
Wash me thoroughly from my iniquity,
And cleanse me from my sin.

For I acknowledge my transgressions,
And my sin is always before me.
Against You, You only, have I sinned,
And done this evil in Your sight—

That You may be found just when You speak,
And blameless when You judge. . . .
Purge me with hyssop, and I shall be clean;
Wash me, and I shall be whiter than snow.
Make me hear joy and gladness,
That the bones You have broken may rejoice.
Hide Your face from my sins,
And blot out all my iniquities.

Create in me a clean heart, O God,
And renew a steadfast spirit within me.
Do not cast me away from Your presence,
And do not take Your Holy Spirit from me.

Restore to me the joy of Your salvation,
And uphold me by Your generous Spirit. . . .

Deliver me from the guilt of bloodshed, O God,
The God of my salvation,
And my tongue shall sing aloud of Your
    righteousness.
O Lord, open my lips,
And my mouth shall show forth Your praise.

For You do not desire sacrifice, or else I would
   give it;
You do not delight in burnt offering.
The sacrifices of God are a broken spirit,
A broken and a contrite heart—
These, O God, You will not despise. . . .

It is interesting to compare these words to those of
another of the psalms—Psalm 1. There is a long way
between Psalms 1 and 51, not in terms of pages in a book
or years of personal experience, but in terms of the distance between obedience and disobedience. Psalm 1 says:

Blessed is the man
Who walks not in the counsel of the ungodly,
Nor stands in the path of sinners,
Nor sits in the seat of the scornful;
But his delight is in the law of the Lord,
And in His law he meditates day and night.
He shall be like a tree
Planted by the rivers of water,
That brings forth its fruit in its season,
Whose leaf also shall not wither;

And whatever he does shall prosper.
The ungodly are not so,
But are like the chaff which the wind drives away.
Therefore the ungodly shall not stand in the
   judgment,
Nor sinners in the congregation of the righteous.
For the Lord knows the way of the righteous,
But the way of the ungodly shall perish.

At one point in his life, David could have been described as the embodiment of the man in Psalm 1, a man like a tree planted by rivers of water. He had taken delight in God's law and meditated on God's Word day and night. In this way, spiritual strength had been forged in David, and all that he touched had been fruitful. But somewhere along the way his attention had been diverted from that Word to a woman, Bathsheba. As a result, he had become like the chaff the wind drives away.

In his mighty fall, David lost not only his integrity, but his joy as well. In Psalm 51, David begs God to cleanse him of his sin, crying: "Make me hear joy and gladness, that the bones You have broken may rejoice.

. . . Restore to me the joy of Your salvation." In his grief, David longed to experience afresh the joy of his salvation.

Though sin often brings immediate pleasure, it gives no lasting joy. If we understand the difference, we can avoid the pitfalls that entice the believer.

The time of greatest joy in my life was my conversion to Christ, the defining moment of my whole life. Compared to that, nothing else in the world is of any value.

I hear that testimony often. My friend John Guest, a British preacher and evangelist, tells of the night he was converted in Liverpool, England. He says that he didn't merely run home, he actually skipped, leaping over fire hydrants along the way. My wife, Vesta, kept waking up during the night following her conversion, pinching herself and asking, "Do I still have it?" Satisfied that she did still have new life in Christ, she would joyously fall back to sleep.

As a new Christian I was infatuated with Scripture. I wanted to spend almost every waking moment reading it. As a result, I made the dean's list in my first semester of college. It was not the list of academic achievement, however; it was the list of students placed on academic probation. I made A's in gym and in Bible, and D's in all the rest of my classes. The A in Bible kept me from flunking out of school.

During those initial months of my Christian life, I was given to enormous mood swings, from tremendous spiritual highs to frightful lows. I visited a minister, seeking counsel. He explained that such a spiritual roller coaster ride was not uncommon for new Christians, and that as I matured in my faith my ups and downs would even out. He also counseled me to look to the Bible and not my feelings as the basis of the Christian life. I've never received wiser counsel.

THE WORD IN CONVERSION

God is pleased to use Scripture to pierce the heart and awaken us to faith. Faith does indeed come by hearing, and hearing by the Word of God (Rom. 10:17). Hebrews 4:12–13 says:

> For the word of God is living and powerful, and sharper than any two-edged sword, piercing even to the division of soul and spirit, and of joints and marrow, and is a discerner of the thoughts and

intents of the heart. And there is no creature hidden from His sight, but all things are naked and open to the eyes of Him to whom we must give account.

History is replete with stories of great people who were converted through the power of the Word. Augustine, living a life of sheer immorality, one day heard children playing a game in which they shouted the refrain, "*Tolle lege, tolle lege,*" Latin for "Take up and read." As he heard this, his eyes fell upon the open text of a Bible, where he read, "Let us walk properly, as in the day, not in revelry and drunkenness, not in lewdness and lust, not in strife and envy. But put on the Lord Jesus Christ, and make no provision for the flesh, to fulfill its lusts" (Rom. 13:13–14). When Augustine read the words, "not in revelry and drunkenness, not in lewdness and lust," he was pierced by the Word of God and made alive by the Spirit of God.

Centuries later, Martin Luther was awakened in similar fashion. Luther had struggled deeply with the justice of God, admitting that at times he hated the very concept. Then, while reading Augustine's commentary on Romans 1:17, Luther suddenly saw the truth of the gospel, that the righteousness of Christ is given by faith alone. This awakening in Luther launched the Protestant Reformation.

Romans also was instrumental in the conversion of John Wesley. He was at a worship service on Aldersgate Street in London on May 24, 1738, when he heard a sermon preached from Romans and felt his heart "strangely warmed." Wesley considered that the moment of his conversion.

My own conversion also was precipitated by the piercing power of Scripture. I was talking with an upperclassman my first week of college. He was the first person I had ever met who spoke of a personal relationship with Jesus. We had a general conversation, with no formal presentation of the gospel, but he spoke of the transcendent wisdom of the Bible. He cited a somewhat obscure passage from Ecclesiastes: "And if a tree falls to the south or the north, in the place where the tree falls, there it shall lie" (11:3b). The words of that text hit me right between the eyes. Suddenly I envisioned myself as the tree, immobile, lying there and simply rotting away. Like the rotting tree I saw my life full of corruption, slowly decaying. With that in my mind, I went to my room and sank to my knees. I knelt beside my bed and begged God to forgive me of my sins. In that moment, I met Christ, who gave me a new life and lifted my rotten soul from the floor of the forest. I think it is probable that in the entire history of the Christian church, I am the only person to have been converted by that verse in Ecclesiastes.

THE WORD IN SPIRITUAL GROWTH

Just as the Word of God is used in conversion, so it is a critical instrument in our spiritual growth. By immersing ourselves in the Word of God, we begin to gain the mind of Christ and learn what discipleship is.

In his second letter to Timothy, the apostle Paul charged his dear friend and disciple to engage in the diligent study of Scripture. It's very important for us to understand the context in which the apostle wrote this admonition. Paul was under a death sentence from the Roman government and was awaiting his imminent execution. Given this situation, his advice to Timothy can be assumed to be that which Paul considered to be of greatest importance. By extension, this advice has enormous relevance for us.

Paul wrote, "Yes, and all who desire to live godly in Christ Jesus will suffer persecution. But evil men and imposters will grow worse and worse, deceiving and being deceived" (2 Tim. 3:12–13). Because Paul was suffering for the gospel, it was only natural for him to speak of persecution. He told Timothy that persecution is the lot of every Christian and the Christian community. Believers must expect it. And what is more, he said, it was not going to get better. Paul was saying to Timothy: "Things are going to get worse and worse, and people are going to come along who are imposters, who will seek to defraud you, to lead you into falsehood, people who will deceive the people of God. But they themselves are deceived."

Deception through distortion of the truth of God is a major problem that confronts every generation and every Christian community. For this reason, the apostle, following after Jesus, was profoundly concerned that Christian people be solidly rooted and grounded in the truth, so that they might not be deceived and led astray by false teaching. He wanted Timothy to be fully equipped in the things of God and in the teachings of Scripture so he would be able to resist such deceptions.

With that background established, Paul was ready to deliver his exhortation. He said to Timothy, "But you must continue in the things which you have learned and been assured of, knowing from whom you have learned them, and that from childhood you have known the Holy Scriptures, which are able to make you wise for salvation through faith which is in Christ Jesus" (2 Tim. 3:14–15).

Paul didn't specify exactly whom he had in mind when he mentioned those who taught Timothy. Was he referring to Timothy's family, especially his grandmother, Lois, and his mother, Eunice, who nurtured Timothy in the faith (2 Tim. 1:5)? Was he referring to himself as Timothy's mentor? Or was Paul directing Timothy's attention to the ultimate source of the things he had learned, namely God? We cannot be sure. But what is clear is what Timothy had learned—the Scriptures. He had been taught the Hebrew Scriptures, our Old Testament, from an early age, and it is clear that Paul wanted Timothy to continue to be a diligent student of the Word of God. It was because of his own study of the Scriptures that Paul was able to say, "I have fought the good fight, I have finished the race, I have kept the faith" (2 Tim. 4:7). In other words, Scripture strengthened Paul to live out the Christian life despite opposition. So it is for us. By continuing to study the Bible, we grow in faith and are able to stand firm in the truth.

The value of Scripture in the life of the believer lies in

its source and its function. In his exhortation to Timothy, Paul commended Scripture to Timothy by saying, "All Scripture is given by inspiration of God, and is profitable for doctrine, for reproof, for correction, for instruction in righteousness" (2 Tim. 3:16).

When I was a little boy, there was a fellow in our community who was a couple of years older than me, and he was something of a bully. He made fun of me and called me names, which hurt my feelings. Sometimes I came home crying to my mother and told her what the other boy had said to upset me. My mother had a favorite response to this. As she wiped away my tears, she said, "When people talk like that about you, son, consider the source."

That little bit of sage advice from my mother was a principle that I learned to a much more intense degree in the academic world. One of the rules of scholarship is to track down in your research the sources for the information you have to make sure that those sources are reliable. Scholars have to be careful not to take anything at face value, because credibility is directly tied to source. They must analyze, examine, and use the critical apparatus at their disposal to track down the real sources.

Paul assured Timothy here that the source of Scripture is God. That Scripture is "given by inspiration" refers not to the way God oversaw the writing of the Bible but to the source of the content of the Bible. The word that is translated "given by inspiration" is the Greek term *theopneust*—literally, "God-breathed." When Paul wrote that Scripture is *God-breathed*, the idea was not one of *inspiration* but of *expiration*; that is, the Bible was *breathed out* by God. The whole point here is that the Bible comes from God. It is His Word and carries with it His authority. Paul wanted Timothy to understand the *source* of the Bible, not the *way* it was inspired.

After stating that the Bible is God-breathed, Paul spelled out its purpose and value. Scripture, he said, is *profitable* for several things, including *doctrine, reproof, correction*, and *instruction in righteousness.*

The value of the Bible lies, first of all, in the fact that it teaches sound doctrine. Though we live in a time when sound teaching is denigrated, the Bible places a high value on it. Much of the New Testament is concerned with doctrine. The teaching ministry is given to the church for building up its people. Paul said, "And He Himself gave some to be apostles, some prophets, some evangelists, and some pastors and teachers, for the equipping of the saints for the work of ministry, for the edifying of the body of Christ" (Eph. 4:11–12).

The Bible is also profitable for reproof and correction, which we as Christians continually need. It is fashionable in some academic circles to exercise scholarly criticism of the Bible. In so doing, scholars place themselves above the Bible and seek to correct it. If indeed the Bible is the Word of God, nothing could be more arrogant. It is *God* who corrects *us;* we don't correct Him. We do not stand over God but under Him.

This yields a practical help for Bible study: read the Bible with a red pen in hand. I suggest that you put a question mark in the margin beside every passage that you find unclear or hard to understand. Likewise, put an X beside every passage that offends you or makes you uncomfortable. Afterward, you can focus on the areas you struggle with, especially the texts marked with an X. This can be a guide to holiness, as the Xs show us quickly where our thinking is out of line with the mind of Christ. If I don't like something I read in Scripture, perhaps I simply don't understand it. If so, studying it again may help. If, in fact, I do understand the passage and still don't like it, this is not an indication there is something wrong with the Bible. It's an indication that something is wrong with *me*, something that needs to change. Often, before we can get something right, we need to first discover what we're doing wrong.

When we experience the "changing of the mind" that is *repentance*, we are not suddenly cleansed of all wrong thinking. The renewing of our minds is a lifelong process. We can accelerate this process by focusing on those passages of Scripture that we don't like. This is part of the "instruction in righteousness" of which Paul speaks.

Finally, Paul explained the overriding purpose for Scripture study. It comes in the final clause, where the apostle wrote, ". . . that the man of God may be complete, thoroughly equipped for every good work." It was as if Paul was warning Timothy that if he neglected the study of God's Word, his life would be incomplete. He would be missing out on this vast resource, this treasury of truth that is the Word of God. And the same is true for us.

GETTING STARTED

The New Testament calls us to a life of discipleship. The word *disciple* means "learner." In any discipline, it is important to begin with the fundamentals and master them. Arnold Palmer once remarked that only about one in fifty amateur golfers holds the club with a proper grip. Legendary football coach Vince Lombardi, when agitated over sloppy play by his players, always called them back to the fundamentals. He would stand before them with a football in his grasp, hold it up for the whole team to see, and say, "This is a football. . . . Am I going too fast?"

Sometimes we chafe at learning the basics. I take violin lessons. My teacher is a highly skilled and accomplished Russian violinist. She worked with me for weeks on how to hold the bow before she would let me actually put the bow on the strings. During that time, I learned more Russian than violin. The word "*nyet*" became a regular part of my vocabulary. I wanted to run before I learned how to walk.

To be sure, the Scriptures call us to maturity. We are not to be satisfied with milk but are to desire the meat of the Word. Hebrews 5:12–14a says:

> For though by this time you ought to be teachers, you need someone to teach you again the first principles of the oracles of God; and you have come to

need milk and not solid food. For everyone who partakes only of milk is unskilled in the word of righteousness, for he is a babe. But solid food belongs to those who are of full age.

I think one of the reasons many Christians never get to the meat of the Word but remain at the milk level is because they never really learned how to drink the milk. There is a reason why scales are important to the piano player and the grip to the golfer. We must master these basics if we are to reach higher levels of proficiency.

Virtually every Christian at some point has resolved to read the entire Bible. If we believe the Bible is the Word of God, it's natural not to want to miss a word of it. If God delivered a letter to your mailbox, I am sure you would read it. But the Bible is a pretty big letter, and its sheer bulk is somewhat daunting, even to the person with the best of intentions. Therefore, few Christians actually keep a resolution to read through the Bible.

At seminars, I often ask for a show of hands indicating how many people have read the entire Bible. Rarely do even 50 percent of the people answer "yes." I ask, "How many of you have read the book of Genesis?" Almost everyone raises his hand. Then I say, "Keep your hand up if you've also read Exodus." Only a few hands are lowered. "Leviticus?" That's when hands start dropping quickly. With Numbers it's even worse.

Reading Genesis is almost like reading a novel. It is mostly narrative history and biography. It tells of important events in the lives of important people such as Noah, Abraham, Jacob, and Joseph. Exodus is likewise gripping, as it tells the poignant story of Israel's enslavement in Egypt and of its liberation under the leadership of Moses. The contest with Pharaoh is exciting. But when we get to Leviticus, everything changes. It's difficult reading about the ceremonies, the sacrifices, and the cleansing rituals because they are foreign to us today. We lack a road map to help us through these difficult portions of the Bible.

When I enrolled in college, I declared myself a history major. That lasted one semester. My first course was History of Civilization, which covered the scope of history from the ancient Sumerians up to the Eisenhower administration. I was quickly lost and confused by the sheer amount of data I tried to assimilate. It was a clear case of information overload. I had no framework in which to process the dates, people, events, and other facts that assaulted my memory bank. I was relieved to get a D for the course and hurried to change my major.

What happened to me in this history class is what happens to many Christians who try to read the Bible from cover to cover. I think there is a better way to go about it. For Christians to truly understand the Bible, they need first to gain an understanding of its basic structure and framework.

Here's my recommendation: begin with an overview of the Bible. Get the basic framework first. If possible, enroll in a class that provides such an overview. At Ligonier Ministries, we have produced an audio and video series titled *Dust to Glory*. It gives the basic structure of the Bible from Genesis to Revelation. It does not go into details, but it covers the high points of redemptive history. In addition to this series, I collaborated with Robert Wolgemuth to produce *What's in the Bible?* The goal of this book is to help the person who has never had a simple introduction to the Bible. In 1977, I published a book titled *Knowing Scripture*, which is designed to help people master the basic rules of biblical interpretation. I frankly think this book is one of the most important helps that I've ever been able to provide for people in studying the Bible, because it provides basic, foundational principles of biblical interpretation to keep people from falling into errors that would lead to distortions of the teaching of Scripture.

Once you understand the basic framework, you are much better equipped to read the Bible. Here is a pattern I recommend for people who have never read the Bible, beginning with the Old Testament:

- ❐ Genesis (the history of Creation, the fall, and God's covenantal dealings with the patriarchs)
- ❐ Exodus (the history of Israel's liberation and formation as a nation)
- ❐ Joshua (the history of the military conquest of the Promised Land)
- ❐ Judges (Israel's transition from a tribal federation to a monarchy)
- ❐ 1 Samuel (Israel's emerging monarchy under Saul and David)
- ❐ 2 Samuel (David's reign)
- ❐ 1 Kings (Solomon and the divided kingdom)
- ❐ 2 Kings (the fall of Israel)
- ❐ Ezra (the Israelites' return from exile)

- ❑ Nehemiah (the restoration of Jerusalem)
- ❑ Amos and Hosea (examples of minor prophets)
- ❑ Jeremiah (an example of a major prophet)
- ❑ Ecclesiastes (Wisdom Literature)
- ❑ Psalms and Proverbs (Hebrew poetry)

The New Testament overview includes:

- ❑ The Gospel of Luke (the life of Jesus)
- ❑ Acts (the early church)
- ❑ Ephesians (an introduction to the teaching of Paul)
- ❑ 1 Corinthians (life in the church)
- ❑ 1 Peter (an introduction to Peter)
- ❑ 1 Timothy (an introduction to the Pastoral Epistles)
- ❑ Hebrews (Christology)
- ❑ Romans (Paul's theology)

By reading these books, a student can get a basic feel for and understanding of the scope of the Bible without getting bogged down in the more difficult sections. From there, he or she can fill in the gaps to complete the reading of the entire Bible.

As a practical matter, you may want to combine your

reading of the Old and New Testaments. It may help to read a certain number of chapters in the Old Testament and then read some in the New until the study is completed. Martin Luther recommended that his students read through the whole Bible every year to keep the winds of the whole blowing through their minds while concentrating on a particular portion of the Bible.

IMPORTANT TOOLS

I think it is important that we have practical aids and helps for the task of studying the Bible. Here are some that any serious student of Scripture should consider.

I highly recommend using a study Bible. My preference is *The Reformation Study Bible*, for which I was the general editor. It's an annotated Bible that includes helpful notes in the margins, at the bottoms of the pages, and in the sidebars to explain the text of Scripture.

For those who want to dig deeper, there are many fine commentaries on the Bible. Theologians and pastors may have multi-volume commentary sets, but the average layman has no need for such detailed explications of Scripture. However, there are excellent single-volume

Bible commentaries that can help you work through difficult passages.

Every student of the Bible should have a complete concordance. A concordance lists every word that appears in a given translation of Scripture and shows where it appears. This can be very helpful. Maybe you will come upon a word such as *propitiation* and will want to figure out what it means in the text. You can turn to your concordance and look up every reference to it in the Bible. By reading those passages, you soon have a good idea of what the concept means. Of course, some words, such as *love*, may have several hundred references, and it might take you a long time to check each one out. But in the main, the concordance helps you keep the whole context of Scripture in front of you.

Another helpful resource is dramatic audio recordings of the Bible. It's a marvelous thing to hear the Word recited in an exciting way. You can spend time in the Bible by listening to somebody read it to you aloud in a way that brings the proper emphasis to the text.

As helpful as these study aids can be, it is important to remember the purpose behind our study. We must read the Bible existentially; that is, we must become involved in what we're reading. We must not just sit back as spectators, learning facts while remaining untouched and unmoved by the text of Scripture. We must ask ourselves what the Word is saying to us as we read. Only by considering this question will we come to the completeness Paul longed to see in Timothy.

Chapter 2

PRAYER

In a small town in Germany, a barber went to his shop early one morning. His name was Peter Beskindorf, but he was known in the village simply as "Master Peter." Soon he was busy shaving one of his regular customers. As he worked, a large man entered his shop. Peter recognized the man immediately as a fugitive who was wanted by the authorities. Indeed, there was a price on the man's head, but Peter said nothing about that.

When Master Peter finished with his client, the big

man sat down in the barber chair and asked for a shave and a haircut. Peter accommodated the visitor's request as he stropped his razor and prepared the lather. He then began shaving the big man, pressing the sharp edge of the blade against the man's neck. Peter knew that with the slightest pressure, he could slit the man's throat and collect the bounty.

But Peter had no intention of carrying out such a grisly deed. He knew the man, for this was not the first time he had visited Peter's shop or sat in his chair. Indeed, the barber not only knew the man, he loved him. More than a customer, the man was Peter's friend, his mentor, and his hero. The man in Peter's barber chair in the village of Wittenberg, Germany, was Martin Luther.

On this day, while shaving Luther, Master Peter said to the great Reformer, "Dr. Luther, would you be willing to teach me how to pray?" Luther replied that he would be delighted to help. With that, the very busy doctor of theology, leader of the Protestant Reformation, retired to his quarters and penned a booklet especially for Peter titled *A Simple Way to Pray*. In that book, Luther offered a treasure trove of helpful advice on prayer, not just for Peter but for all believers.

WHY SHOULD WE PRAY?

Before we consider Luther's advice on *how* we ought to pray, we should address a more fundamental question: *Why* should we pray? Of the many legitimate answers to this question, we will focus particularly on three. We should pray because prayer is a *duty* of every Christian; because prayer is a *privilege*; and because prayer is a powerful *means of grace*.

Prayer as a Duty

The Bible makes it abundantly clear that God's people are called to be people of prayer. The Old Testament contains numerous examples of men and women who prayed fervently. We think, for example, of Hannah, who begged the Lord for a son:

> Then Elkanah her husband said to her, "Hannah, why do you weep? Why do you not eat? And why is your heart grieved? Am I not better to you than ten sons?"
>
> So Hannah arose after they had finished eating and drinking in Shiloh. Now Eli the priest

was sitting on the seat by the doorpost of the tabernacle of the LORD. And she was in bitterness of soul, and prayed to the LORD and wept in anguish. Then she made a vow and said, "O LORD of hosts, if You will indeed look on the affliction of Your maidservant and remember me, and not forget Your maidservant, but will give Your maidservant a male child, then I will give him to the LORD all the days of his life, and no razor shall come upon his head."

And it happened, as she continued praying before the LORD, that Eli watched her mouth. Now Hannah spoke in her heart; only her lips moved, but her voice was not heard. Therefore Eli thought she was drunk. So Eli said to her, "How long will you be drunk? Put your wine away from you!"

But Hannah answered and said, "No, my lord, I am a woman of sorrowful spirit. I have drunk neither wine nor intoxicating drink, but have poured out my soul before the LORD. Do not consider your maidservant a wicked woman, for out of the abundance of my complaint and grief I have spoken until now."

Then Eli answered and said, "Go in peace, and the God of Israel grant your petition which you have asked of Him."

And she said, "Let your maidservant find favor in your sight." So the woman went her way and ate, and her face was no longer sad. (1 Sam. 1:8–18)

After God answered Hannah's prayer, she prayed again, this time a prayer of thanksgiving. It bears a remarkable similarity to the Magnificat, the exultant prayer of Mary, the mother of Jesus (compare 1 Sam. 2:1–10 and Luke 1:46–55).

Hannah's prayer is but a single example of the multitude of prayers recorded in the Old Testament. The Psalms contain an entire collection of prayers by David and others. The New Testament also bears witness to the regular custom of prayer among believers, and especially by Jesus Himself. Since prayer was characteristic of our biblical forebears, it should be normative for us, as well.

Beyond these examples, we have the explicit commands given to us by the apostles and by Jesus. The apostle Paul frequently urges his readers to be diligent in their prayer lives. For example, he says:

. . . rejoicing in hope, patient in tribulation, continuing steadfastly in prayer. (Rom. 12:12)

Do not deprive one another except with consent for a time, that you may give yourselves to fasting and prayer; and come together again so that Satan does not tempt you because of your lack of self-control. (1 Cor. 7:5)

Be anxious for nothing, but in everything by prayer and supplication, with thanksgiving, let your requests be made known to God. (Phil. 4:6)

. . . for it is sanctified by the word of God and prayer. (1 Tim. 4:5)

Jesus tells us to pray always and not give up. He made this clear in the parable of the unjust judge:

Then He spoke a parable to them, that men always ought to pray and not lose heart, saying: "There was in a certain city a judge who did not fear God nor regard man. Now there was a widow in that city;

and she came to him, saying, 'Get justice for me from my adversary.' And he would not for a while; but afterward he said within himself, 'Though I do not fear God nor regard man, yet because this widow troubles me I will avenge her, lest by her continual coming she weary me.'"

Then the Lord said, "Hear what the unjust judge said." (Luke 18:1–6)

In this parable, our Lord speaks of something that we "ought" to do (namely, to pray always). The word *ought* describes an ethical or moral necessity. Whatever Jesus says we "ought" to do becomes a solemn duty for us to perform. Prayer is one such duty.

Prayer as a Privilege

The obligation or duty of prayer is balanced by the fact that it is also a privilege. When Paul speaks of the consequences of our justification, he writes, "Therefore, having been justified by faith, we have peace with God through our Lord Jesus Christ, through whom also we have access by faith into this grace in which we stand, and rejoice in hope of the glory of God" (Rom. 5:1–2).

In the Old Testament, "access" to God was limited by virtue of the separation between the Holy Place and the Holy of Holies in the temple. Of course, believers could pray, but they were kept a certain distance from the glorious presence of God. Only the high priest, one day out of the year, was permitted to enter the Holy of Holies. A thick curtain called the wall of separation guarded the entrance. But when Jesus was crucified, an earthquake struck Jerusalem, and in its upheaval that curtain was torn apart. The atoning death of Christ gave us a new, freer kind of access to the Father. Christ won for us peace with God and the end of estrangement. We are now invited to enter by our prayers into the Holy of Holies. What a great privilege.

Christianity is not an exercise in mysticism. The usual goal of mystical religions is to reach spiritual unity with God. The desire is often expressed in terms of being "one with the universe" (or some other object). The goal is for the individual's identity to merge with the whole, like a drop of water that falls *into* the ocean and eventually can no longer be distinguished *from* the ocean.

Such mysticism is radically different from Christianity. The Christian faith never sees our goal as *becoming*

God or as losing our individual identity by being *swallowed up in* God. The goal of spiritual growth is not the kind of union with God that destroys our personalities. Instead, it is a special spiritual union in which rich *communion* takes place. The word *communion* is composed of the prefix "com," which simply means "with," and the root word "union." So communion with Christ flows out of union with Him. And the essence of communion is prayer.

Paul uses the metaphor of marriage to illustrate this communion, depicting Christ as the Bridegroom and the church as His bride. Paul writes:

> Husbands, love your wives, just as Christ also loved the church and gave Himself for her, that He might sanctify and cleanse her with the washing of water by the word, that He might present her to Himself a glorious church, not having spot or wrinkle or any such thing, but that she should be holy and without blemish. So husbands ought to love their own wives as their own bodies; he who loves his wife loves himself. No one ever hated his own flesh, but nourishes and cherishes it, just as

the Lord does the church. For we are members of His body, of His flesh and of His bones. "For this reason a man shall leave his father and mother and be joined to his wife, and the two shall become one flesh." This is a great mystery, but I speak concerning Christ and the church. Nevertheless, let each one of you in particular so love his own wife as himself, and let the wife see that she respects her husband. (Eph. 5:25–33)

There are several aspects of the relationship between the bride and the groom that illustrate aspects of our relationship to Jesus. First, marriage is seen as two people making gifts of themselves to one another. In the standard marriage liturgy in the church, there is a moment when the bride is "given away." The minister says, "Who gives this woman to be married to this man?" The bride's father, having escorted her down the aisle, responds, "I do" or "Her mother and I do." The bride is depicted as a donation, a gift. Likewise, the heavenly Father gives the church to Christ as His bride (John 6:37). Christ then gives Himself for her. So the union between the Christian and Christ is based on Christ's gift of Himself for the believer. And not only does He give Himself, but the Holy Spirit gives the supreme gift by which the person is united to Christ, the gift of faith. The whole basis for our relationship to God is grace. It is not something we earn or deserve or purchase. It is a gift.

Second, marriage is seen as producing the most intimate kind of union that two human beings can have. The institution and structure of marriage is under attack in our culture today, and many young people have dismissed the sanctity of marriage and chosen to live together without entering into this covenant relationship. However, some young couples who choose to live together find this arrangement far from satisfying, and they come to the church and say, "We want to get married." They want to take that extra step because they realize marriage will take them to a deeper dimension of union than they can find just by living together. But the believer's union with Christ is deeper still.

If you are outside of a room and you want to enter that room, you have to cross a threshold. You go through the door, and when you walk across that threshold, you are moving from outside the room into the room. After the transition has been made, once you've walked through the door, you are in the room. In order to be *in* the room, you first have to move *into* the room from outside of it. That's a simple distinction, but it's important. The New Testament tells us to believe *in* Christ and calls us to faith *in* Christ, but the word that it uses is the Greek word *eis*, which literally means "into," so the New Testament literally is calling us to believe *into* Christ. Once we believe into Christ and embrace Christ, then we are indwelt by the Holy Spirit, who is, in reality, Christ in us. So the mystical union is that once we are born of the Spirit and are given the gift of faith and move into Christ, then we are in Christ and Christ is in us.

This union with Christ, in turn, is the foundation for all of Christian unity. If I am in Christ and you are in Christ, then we are both, right now, spiritually united in Him. We may be at odds with each other as Christians; we may disagree in our theology. Nevertheless, we enjoy a transcendent unity by virtue of our spiritual union with Christ.

I hear it said all the time in ecumenical discussions that we are called to pursue organizational unity with other Christians because Jesus, in His High Priestly Prayer, prayed "that they may be one, as We are" (John

17:11b). It is said that we've got to help make Jesus' prayer come to pass. But in a very real sense, that prayer has been answered already, because we have a transcendent spiritual unity with every Christian in this world. I am in Christ and they are in Christ, and Christ is in all of us. So believers' union with Christ is the foundation for their relationship with Him.

Third, marriage involves not just union but communion. When we talk about communion, we're talking about the communication that takes place between people. That's why the Apostles' Creed talks about "the communion of saints," which is the communion believers have with each other. But far more important is our communion with Christ Himself, which takes place through the means of prayer.

One of the common problems experienced by people who are having trouble in their marriages is a breakdown in communication, and one of the complaints I often hear from wives is this: "My husband never talks to me." When communication fails, the basic communion between two people breaks down, and it is no different with our relationship to Christ. If Christ were to make a complaint, it would be, "My bride doesn't talk to me; she has missed the opportunity for prayer and communion that I established with her." Such a complaint would be completely valid because we all fail to take full advantage of the privilege of prayer in order to commune with Christ. When we do this, our communion with Him is disrupted.

Fourth, marriage involves mutual delight in each other and an ongoing persistent state of affection. Two people who have an ardent, passionate affection for each other take delight in being with each other and in each other's presence.

My wife, Vesta, and I went together for eight years before we were married, and for six of those eight years we were at different schools, so we communicated by telephone or by letter. I wrote to Vesta every single day during that time and she wrote me every day because we wanted to stay in profound communication. We didn't write those letters because we had to. We wrote those letters because we wanted to. I wanted to express to her my affection for her and my desire to be close to her, and she wrote to me for the same reasons. Our letters weren't newsletters, they were love letters.

That's what prayer is. It's a communication of love from the bride to the Bridegroom. It's not enough to pray because we ought to pray; beyond the duty element, there should be a delight about being engaged in this kind of communication. What a privilege prayer is.

Prayer as a Means

We pray not only because it is our duty and our privilege, but also because prayer is a powerful means by which God brings His will to pass.

Does prayer change things? We must answer with a resounding "Yes." Prayer changes *us* and prayer changes *things*. James 5:13–18 teaches us:

> Is anyone among you suffering? Let him pray. Is anyone cheerful? Let him sing psalms. Is anyone among you sick? Let him call for the elders of the church, and let them pray over him, anointing him with oil in the name of the Lord. And the prayer of faith will save the sick, and the Lord will raise him up. And if he has committed sins, he will be forgiven. Confess your trespasses to one another, and pray for one another, that you may be healed. The effective, fervent prayer of a righteous man avails much. Elijah was a man with a nature like

ours, and he prayed earnestly that it would not rain; and it did not rain on the land for three years and six months. And he prayed again, and the heaven gave rain, and the earth produced its fruit.

This passage teaches that "the fervent prayer of a righteous man avails much." To "avail much" means *to make a significant impact.* This prayer is *effective.* It has real power.

Thus, prayer is a *means* that God uses to bring about His intended *ends.* Just as God uses the preaching of the gospel as the power unto salvation, so He uses the power of prayer to bring about redemption. Our prayers cannot force God to do anything, but He uses them as His own instruments to bring about His will.

Monica, the mother of Augustine, was a devout Christian woman. When Augustine was a young man, he was unconverted and wayward, and Monica grieved deeply over his unbridled sin. Monica prayed with tears every day for his conversion. On one occasion, she visited her pastor, the famous Archbishop Ambrose of Milan, looking for comfort and some assurance that her prayers were not in vain. Ambrose sought to comfort her with a rhetorical question: "Monica, could a child of so many tears possibly be lost?"

The answer Ambrose intended to his question was "No." He assumed that any child whose mother prayed for him so faithfully would come into a state of grace eventually. I disagree. The tearful prayers of a grieving mother do not guarantee her child's conversion. However, the probability of it is high, at least high enough to provide great comfort. I might preach with passion and tears, only to see no one converted, but I know that in the final analysis God's Word will not return to Him void. In like manner, the prayers of His people are never wasted. Prayer works, and that is a tremendous incentive to pray.

HOW SHOULD WE PRAY?

Many years ago, I heard a sermon in which the minister gave a detailed description of starving people around the world. When he reached the crescendo point of his sermon, he leaned over the pulpit and said, "Now you people have to do something about this." I remember walking out of the room feeling guilty but also feeling a bit befuddled because I didn't know what to do. So many times that's what we ministers do to people. We tell them, "You ought to do this or that." We lay guilt trips on them, but we never show them how to do what we are exhorting them to do.

I don't think there is any area of the Christian life in which people are more weighed down by guilt than in the area of their prayer lives. Most Christians will readily confess that their prayer lives are not what they should be. And one major reason for this problem is that Christians don't really know how to pray effectively.

Master Peter did not ask Luther to teach him *why* he should pray; he wanted to know *how* he should pray. This was the same question the disciples asked Jesus. Obviously they had noticed a link between the extraordinary power of Jesus and His prayer life. Jesus answered their request by providing them, and us, with what we call the Lord's Prayer:

> Now it came to pass, as He was praying in a certain place, when He ceased, that one of His disciples said to Him, "Lord, teach us to pray, as John also taught his disciples."

So He said to them, "When you pray, say:
Our Father in heaven,
Hallowed be Your name.
Your kingdom come.
Your will be done
On earth as it is in heaven.
Give us day by day our daily bread.
And forgive us our sins,
For we also forgive everyone who is indebted to us.
And do not lead us into temptation,
But deliver us from the evil one." (Luke 11:1–4)

The Lord's Prayer is a model. It gives us not only an actual prayer to pray, but also a pattern to follow in prayer.

Consider the first phrase. The prayer begins with a personal form of address in which God is called "Father." This was a radical thing in Jesus' day, because Jews did not address God as "Father." But not only did Jesus constantly call Him "Father," He invited us to do the same.

The first petition is that the name of God might be regarded as holy. From there, Jesus moves to a request for the kingdom of God to triumph. We are to pray for His kingdom to come and the will of God to be done on earth as it already is done in heaven.

I've often wondered whether there is a logical link between the first petition of the Lord's Prayer and the next two. If so, we must conclude that until the name of God is regarded as holy, we cannot expect to see His kingdom come or His will be done on the earth as it is in heaven, where God is surrounded by the seraphim who continually sing, "Holy, holy, holy."

So we need to begin our prayers by bowing in reverence before our God, acknowledging Him as our loving and holy heavenly Father. And just as the Lord's Prayer emphasizes the kingdom of God and His glory, so should our prayers. This means praying beyond our own circumstances and needs—seeing the bigger picture and praying for God's work in the rest of the world.

PRACTICAL SUGGESTIONS

A few years ago, Dr. Archie Parrish, the founder and president of SERVE International, led a seminar in our church on what is called "kingdom-focused prayer." In this seminar, we learned that instead of spending most of our time in prayer telling the Lord what we would like for ourselves, the focus of our prayer needs to be on the work of Christ and the work of the kingdom, so that we begin to pray earnestly and specifically for the effective impact of the gospel in the world in which we live. As a practical guide for this prayer enterprise, Archie published a booklet wherein he comments on Luther's *A Simple Way to Pray*. More than anything else I've ever encountered, this little book has changed the way I pray. It offers numerous practical suggestions for structuring one's prayer life. For instance:

• Luther suggested to Master Peter that he set aside time for prayer every day. Because pressures frequently threaten to disrupt our prayer time, it is helpful to have a regular time or times scheduled.

• The Reformer also suggested that, like Jesus, Peter go apart to a quiet place where it would be easier to concentrate. Luther told him: "Prayer is like your task as a barber. The last thing I want you to do is to have your mind wandering when you've lathered up my face and you take out that blade and start shaving me. I don't want you to start wool-gathering and end up slitting my throat."

• Luther also recommended that Peter pray out loud. There is something helpful about articulating communication to the Lord aloud. Luther suggested emulating Jesus, who prayed out loud when He was in the Garden of Gethsemane, even though He was by Himself.

Perhaps the richest suggestion I gleaned from Luther's booklet is to pray "through" three things: the Lord's Prayer, the Ten Commandments, and the Apostles' Creed. There is an important difference between *praying* the Lord's Prayer and *praying through* the Lord's Prayer. To pray through the Lord's Prayer is to focus attention on each of the petitions for a time. For example, instead of simply praying, "Hallowed be Your name," I might say: "O Lord, we live in an age where Your name is not only not revered or honored but is used as profanity. Bring such an awakening to Your glory that no one would think of dragging Your name through the mud or treating it as common or trivial. Let it be on our lips and in our hearts as an expression of our adoration for You. Give me grace to always respect Your sacred name in my heart and with my lips."

Then, of course, I go on to the next petitions of the Lord's Prayer: "Your kingdom come. Your will be done on earth as it is in heaven." Again, I expand on this thought, making it personal.

As I pray these petitions, I think about the mission of the church. I think about my responsibility as a Christian to bear witness to the lordship of Christ. I think about the things that we are engaged in at our local church, in the work of Ligonier Ministries, or in the outreach of other ministries. I then begin to pray specifically about ways in which the kingdom of God can be enriched and strengthened by ministry activities and programs that we're engaged in or that we know about. I pray with specific reference to missionaries, for example, or other programs that are designed to extend the kingdom.

The idea is to go right on through the Lord's Prayer, asking for your daily bread, for forgiveness of your sins, and for a forgiving spirit within yourself, all the way down to the "amen." Luther said the amen is very important because we are told to pray with faith. The word *amen* is derived from the Hebrew word for "truth," so when we say "amen" at the end of the Lord's Prayer, or of any prayer, we are saying, "This is true, I'm committed to this, and I believe what I've just said to you, O God."

Now, it could easily take quite a bit of time to go

through each of the petitions of the Lord's Prayer and focus your attention on them and expand them in this way. Luther recognized that, so he told his barber that he would sometimes go through only one or two petitions because his mind would be so engaged and he would become fervently concerned about the petition before him. That's OK, he said, because we're simply looking for "pegs" on which to hang our thoughts, as it were, as we engage in focused prayer.

Luther also suggested praying through the Ten Commandments. His method was to think first about what the law was teaching him, the instruction found in each of the commandments. Then he reflected on his gratitude for the law and for what each of the commandments does. For instance, when he came to the fifth commandment, "Honor your father and your mother" (Ex. 20:11a), Luther tried to express his gratitude, not only for what his parents had done for him, but for what Prince Frederick of Saxony, who was his authority, did for him. Next he turned to confession, allowing the commandments to show him where he had sinned and where he needed to make confession. Finally, he would pray through the law with a kingdom focus, asking that the Lord's name would be hallowed, that the world would be rid of idols, that the singular majesty of God would be so visible that there would be no other gods competing with Him, and so forth.

Finally, Luther suggested praying through the Apostle's Creed, which begins by saying, "I believe in God the Father Almighty, maker of heaven and earth, and in Jesus Christ, His only Son, our Lord." Each phrase of the creed would focus his attention on a matter for prayer.

And so, instead of a willy-nilly, ad hoc, unorganized, woolgathering process of praying, Luther laid out a biblical map to follow, a methodology that focuses our attention on our communication with the Lord.

Another simple way to structure prayer is by using the acrostic ACTS. The letters stand for *adoration, confession, thanksgiving,* and *supplication.* I use this structure for pastoral prayers in church. It keeps me focused on the vital elements that every prayer should contain. So often our prayers are limited to personal appeals for whatever blessings we would like to receive from God or requests for our friends and relatives. We learn this at an early age when we pray, "God bless Mommy, Daddy, sister, brother, Grandma. . . ." Of course, it is good to pray for family members, friends, and those in need. But we need to understand that prayer is more than supplication and intercession.

I confess I am surprised by Jesus' answer to the disciples' request that He teach them how to pray. I would have expected Him to say something like this: "If you want to master the art of prayer, immerse yourself in the Psalms—prayers that were inspired by the Holy Spirit." Or He might have directed them to the recorded prayers of saints such as Hannah or Nehemiah. Instead, He gave them a model for communicating with God that has inspired, comforted, and strengthened Christians for two thousand years. But whether we use as our model the Lord's Prayer, the Ten Commandments, the Apostles' Creed, ACTS, or something else altogether, the important thing is that we *pray*.

Personally, I will be forever grateful to that barber in Wittenberg for daring to ask Luther to teach him how to pray. Thanks to his request and Luther's simple answer, multitudes have dug deeper into the life of prayer.

Chapter 3

WORSHIP

The father of the two boys was bursting with pride. It was one thing to have a son follow in his footsteps; it was quite another to have two. The father was a minister, and he was watching the ordination of his sons to that same ministry.

The young ministers were zealous for their work. In their zeal, they decided to experiment, to add something new to the worship service. What happened was far from what they expected. Not only did God disapprove of their innovations, He manifested His disapproval by killing them on the spot. This dreadful event is recorded in Leviticus 10:1–3:

> Then Nadab and Abihu, the sons of Aaron, each took his censer and put fire in it, put incense on it, and offered profane fire before the LORD, which He had not commanded them. So fire went out from the LORD and devoured them, and they died before the LORD. And Moses said to Aaron, "This is what the LORD spoke, saying:
> 'By those who come near Me
> I must be regarded as holy;
> And before all the people I must be glorified.'"
> So Aaron held his peace.

This grim episode in the history of ancient Israel makes an unforgettable point: *worship of the living God is serious business.* It is not something to be trifled with or taken lightly. God is serious about how we worship Him, and we must be serious about it, too. Unfortunately, we tend to follow the example of Nadab and Abihu, trying to come to God on our own terms.

I experienced culture shock when I enrolled in the

Free University of Amsterdam in the Netherlands and went to my first class with Professor G. C. Berkouwer. Dr. Berkouwer came in from the side door, and immediately every student in the amphitheater stood at attention. He walked to the podium and nodded, and only then did the students take their seats. He then opened his notebook and proceeded to deliver his lecture without interruption. No student dared to raise his hand or ask a question. At the end of his lecture, he closed his book and turned toward the door. As he did, the students again stood as he walked out. This was the way people in that culture showed respect to the clergy or professors.

On one unusually warm day, I was sitting at the back of the amphitheater. It was so hot that I took off my coat (we always had to wear a coat and tie). At that point, Dr. Berkouwer stopped in mid-sentence, looked straight at me, and said, "Would the American please put his coat back on?" He did not yet know me, but he knew I had to be an American. Only an American would have dared insult him by taking off his coat in the presence of the professor.

Because we Americans have proclaimed our independence from monarchs, we tend to have little respect for sovereignty or authority of any sort. We don't know much about paying homage or following proper etiquette, particularly when we come into the presence of our King. But we need to learn, because every worship service we attend is an audience with the King of kings.

REGULATED BY GOD

Worship was one of the key points of disagreement during the Protestant Reformation. The Reformation produced a very strong concern that God be worshiped properly. The Reformers objected to the ways in which worship was conducted in the medieval Roman Catholic Church. In the British Isles, the Reformation eventually produced the non-Conformists, or Puritans, whose conflict with the Church of England focused on worship. The Reformers and Puritans responded to what they saw as deviations from the instructions for worship handed down in Scripture. Since we count ourselves as their theological descendants, we, too, must look to Scripture to determine what is good and proper in worship.

We can draw our initial cues for understanding proper worship from the Ten Commandments. The first four commandments, usually called the "first table of the law," concentrate on our responsibilities toward God. The very first commandment says, "You shall have no other gods before Me" (Ex. 20:3).

Now, let's pause for a moment. We've all heard the Ten Commandments. Some of us have memorized them. But have we ever considered why this commandment is first? Why does the Decalogue start with this particular law? The fact that God, in giving these laws, started here indicates to me that there is some level of priority, some level of supreme importance, to this commandment.

Consider the words God uses here: "You shall have no other gods before Me." The word *before* is critical. God is not saying, "You can have all kinds of other deities as long as they don't rank ahead of me; I only want to be judged to be first in importance." On the contrary, "before Me" means "in My presence." God's presence is ubiquitous; He is everywhere. So God is saying, "I will not tolerate any other gods." Thus, the first commandment of the law guards against all forms of idolatry, because idolatry misdirects worship from the true God to some kind of substitute, a fraudulent deity.

In the first chapter of Romans, the apostle Paul

declares that from the beginning of creation God has revealed Himself plainly in nature. This self-revelation to every human being unveils God's eternal power and deity. Paul declares that in every moment of our existence we are in a theater in which an ongoing revelation of God's nature and character is playing out before our eyes. We, as God's creatures, have knowledge of who He really is. But Paul goes on to say that the universal sin of fallen humanity is to take the knowledge that God reveals and suppress it, then to exchange it for a lie, choosing to worship and serve the creature rather than the Creator. The fundamental sin of the human race, according to Paul, is that despite knowing God, men do not honor Him as God; rather, they engage in idolatry. Therefore, it is really no surprise that at the very beginning of the law, God pronounced a commandment to guard against this basic human tendency to substitute an idol for the truth about God.

When we take up the question of worship, we have to keep before us at all times the understanding that God is a jealous God, that He absolutely requires human beings to honor, glorify, and worship Him in the way He commands, not according to the ways we prefer. If anything comes screaming out of the pages of sacred Scripture, it is that God commands us to worship Him according to His law and not according to our own ideas. This is the first principle of worship we need to know, because if left to ourselves, given our universal behavioral pattern as fallen creatures, we not only will gravitate toward some form of idolatry, we will be swept into it.

The problem with idolatry is that it involves producing a substitute for the true God. Although we don't make idols of stone and wood anymore, we are all too prone to take the biblical revelation of God, look at those attributes of God that we find distasteful, such as His sovereignty, holiness, justice, and wrath, and toss them aside. We then construct a god who is all love, grace, and mercy. In other words, we create a god who is not God. That god is an idol. But the only God we are to worship is the God who reveals Himself in sacred Scripture, and true worship focuses on the whole counsel of God, not on isolated aspects of God with which we are comfortable.

Consider also the second commandment: "You shall not make for yourself a carved image" (Ex. 20:4a). This commandment strongly reinforces the first commandment, so that the very first two commandments of the

Decalogue protect worship and give us guidelines for that worship.

IN SPIRIT AND IN TRUTH

Another portion of Scripture that gives tremendous insight into proper worship is John 4, where we find the story of Jesus' conversation with the Samaritan woman at the well in Sychar. In the midst of this discussion, the woman said to Jesus: "Sir, I perceive that You are a prophet. Our fathers worshiped on this mountain, and you Jews say that in Jerusalem is the place where one ought to worship" (vv. 19–20).

The woman was referring to the different locations for worship that were specified for Jews and Samaritans. The Jews' central sanctuary was in Jerusalem. On festival occasions, the people would come from all over Israel to Jerusalem for the purpose of worship. But the Samaritans, who had no dealings with the Jews, had their own central sanctuary on Mount Gerizim, which overlooked Jacob's Well. Excited to be talking with a man who was obviously a prophet, this woman decided to settle the ancient controversy between the Samaritans and the Jews. So she asked Jesus where people ought to worship. Was it Jerusalem or Mount Gerizim? Which was the proper place for worship?"

But Jesus took the conversation in a different direction. He was not content to answer her "where" question. Instead, He focused on the "how" question. Jesus said: "Woman, believe Me, the hour is coming when you will neither on this mountain, nor in Jerusalem, worship the Father. You worship what you do not know; we know what we worship, for salvation is of the Jews" (vv. 21–22). This was a strong rebuke of the Samaritans' departure from the Jewish faith. The Samaritans had intermarried with pagans and developed a religion of syncretism, blending pagan elements together with the elements of Jewish worship. When Jesus said, "You worship what you do not know," He was saying the Samaritans did not know what they were doing in their worship. They were engaged in worship that was grounded in ignorance or in falsehood.

When Paul came to the magnificent city of Athens, he was not impressed with its high culture. Instead, as the book of Acts tells us, he was "provoked" in his spirit because he saw that the whole city was given to idolatry. When he was invited to address the philosophers at the Areopagus, he confronted the people for their false religion. Having noticed a monument inscribed to "The unknown god," he said, "The One whom you worship without knowing, Him I proclaim to you: God, who made the world and everything in it" (Acts 17:23b–24a). So the Athenians received the same rebuke from the apostle Paul that the Samaritans received from the lips of Jesus. Both of them were saying, in essence, "You people don't even know who it is that you're worshiping because at the heart of your worship is ignorance." God is never pleased with ignorant worship, with worship that is not grounded in the knowledge of God.

Continuing to address the Samaritan woman, Jesus said, "The hour is coming, and now is, when the true worshipers will worship the Father in spirit and truth; for the Father is seeking such to worship Him" (John 4:23). With these words, Jesus announced that God was actually seeking worshipers. We usually think about people seeking God, but here Jesus spoke about God seeking people. And what was God searching for? Jesus said He was seeking *true* worshipers. These words indicated that there is a difference between true worship and false worship, and the difference is determined by the two criteria that

Jesus set forth: *spirit* and *truth*. The Father, Jesus said, was searching for people who would worship Him correctly, who would honor Him as God, who would put aside all forms of idolatry and worship Him the way He commands that He be worshiped—in spirit and truth. Jesus repeated this emphasis in the next verse, saying, "God is Spirit, and those who worship Him must worship in spirit and truth." The key word here is *must*. God Himself has placed an obligation on us to worship Him in spirit and in truth. We must worship God in this way.

What does it mean to worship in spirit and truth? Understanding Jesus' meaning behind the word *spirit* is more difficult than determining what He meant by *truth*. Remember that the discussion here focused initially on the "where" question. The woman was saying, "Where should we worship God—Jerusalem or Mount Gerizim?" One of the things Jesus was teaching her, and us by extension, is that God's presence cannot be confined to a physical location. The woman seems to have assumed that God could be worshiped properly in one location only—if He was to be worshiped at Mount Gerizim, He couldn't be worshiped at Jerusalem, or vice versa. Jesus denied this limitation because God is omnipresent. God is everywhere, so we can worship Him anywhere. We are not restricted to one particular place. That is part of what Jesus was saying by mandating worship in spirit.

Jesus was not saying that we should worship God *only* with our spirits. He was not telling us to send our souls off to worship while allowing our bodies to sleep in or go to the golf course. Rather, He was getting at the fact that since we are created as a unity of body and soul, we can do things in an external, physical way that are distanced or divorced from our minds or our souls. This was the great problem in Israel in the Old Testament. The prophets testified on many occasions that the people would show up physically for worship and would go through the rituals properly, but their souls were somewhere else, as it were. They weren't participating from the depths of their beings. Thus, the prophet Isaiah said, "These people draw near with their mouths and honor Me with their lips, but have removed their hearts far from Me" (Isa. 29:13b). Worship had degenerated into externalism or formalism, just outward activity.

So Jesus was saying, "I want people who, when they come to worship Me, come with their hearts fully engaged with what they are doing." Worship that pleases God is not given grudgingly, out of a mere sense of duty to show up at church on Sunday morning, but it is motivated and driven by a soul that delights in the presence of God. Spiritual worship is worship that is offered by a person who takes delight in honoring God, in praying to God, in listening to the Word of God with his mind fully engaged. This was the posture of the psalmist, who said, "I was glad when they said to me, 'Let us go into the house of the LORD'" (Ps. 122:1).

The Westminster Confession of Faith, Chapter 21, deals with prescriptions for worship, and it says that worship services should contain the sound preaching of the Word of God, but also the conscientious or diligent *hearing* of the Word of God. It is saying that the true worshiper is one whose heart is engaged and who is involved body and soul in the entire experience of worship. Whether it be the singing, the prayers, the sermon, or any other part of the service, he is engaged inwardly in his spirit.

It is much easier to understand what Jesus means when He says that worship that is pleasing and acceptable to God is offered in *truth*. We live in an age that downplays the importance of truth, emphasizing fellowship and emotional experience. Truth means getting at who

God really is, and God is most fully revealed in Jesus, who said, "I am the truth" (John 14:6). How can someone say he loves God but not care about truth? I hear people say, "Doctrine divides." Of course doctrine divides, but it also unites. It unites the ones who love God's truth and are willing to worship Him according to that truth. God wants people to worship Him from the heart and from a mind that is informed of who He is by His Word.

PREPARATION FOR WORSHIP

It is very important that we take time to prepare our hearts to worship God before we set foot in the sanctuary on Sunday morning. God made this clear amid the awesome circumstances of the giving of the law in Exodus 19. God called the people to prepare to come into His presence, or *near* His presence, but not actually onto the mountain where He would speak to Moses. "Then the LORD said to Moses, 'Go to the people and consecrate them today and tomorrow, and let them wash their clothes. And let them be ready for the third day. For on the third day the LORD will come down upon Mount Sinai in the sight of all the people'" (Ex. 19:10–11). God wanted the people of Israel, before they came near to Him, to *get ready* to come near to Him, to *prepare* themselves for an encounter with Him.

Our church service begins at 10:30 a.m. At 10:20, we turn the lights down and begin the prelude. This is the signal for our people to begin preparing for worship. By contrast, God gave Israel two days to prepare. He required them to be consecrated and to wash their clothes. These preparations were appropriate for what was about to happen. If I told my congregation that in three days God was going to appear visibly and that He wanted them to wash their clothes for the occasion, I am sure they would do it. It would seem to be an insignificant requirement for the awesome privilege of standing in God's physical presence.

Exodus 19:14 tells us that Moses did exactly as God commanded; He went down and sanctified the people. The people also obeyed by washing their clothes. They took the time to prepare for worship. We should do the same by reading God's Word and praying for His assistance to worship Him rightly.

Part of our preparation for worship ought to be reminding ourselves of who God is—the holy, sovereign Lord. Turning again to Exodus 19, we read in verse 16:

Then it came to pass on the third day, in the morning, that there were thunderings and lightnings, and a thick cloud on the mountain; and the sound of the trumpet was very loud, so that all the people who were in the camp trembled.

When the trumpet sounded and the moment arrived for the people of Israel to draw near to God, every person in the camp trembled. Unfortunately, few people respond to God in worship like that anymore. Many have forgotten how to tremble before Him, for they do not regard Him as holy. How different their response would be if they could see Him as He revealed Himself to the Israelites:

And Moses brought the people out of the camp to meet with God, and they stood at the foot of the mountain. Now, Mount Sinai was completely in smoke, because the LORD descended upon it in fire. Its smoke ascended like the smoke of a furnace, and the whole mountain quaked greatly. (Ex. 19:17–18)

Over and over again God invited the people, "Come near to Me." But that invitation was balanced by what

God said following the deaths of Nadab and Abihu: "By those who come near Me I must be regarded as holy." We are commanded by God to come into His presence—to come near to *Him*. Not only that, we may come *boldly* into His presence, as Hebrews 4:16 makes clear. But there is a difference between coming *boldly* into the presence of God and coming *arrogantly*. When we come boldly into His presence and draw near to Him, we must always remember that we are to regard Him as holy.

We also must remember that we have no right to come into God's presence on our own. No amount of preparation that we can do is enough to make us fit. We need to be prepared, as the author of Hebrews makes clear:

> Therefore, brethren, having boldness to enter the Holiest by the blood of Jesus, by a new and living way which He consecrated for us, through the veil, that is, His flesh, and having a High Priest over the house of God, let us draw near with a true heart in full assurance of faith, having our hearts sprinkled from an evil conscience and our bodies washed with pure water. (Heb. 10:19–22)

This passage is packed with imagery. First, what is the veil, through which we have gained access to God? It is not the veil that hung in the temple. That veil concealed the glory of God from human sight, but on the day of Christ's crucifixion, the veil of the temple was torn. The author of Hebrews is speaking here of the flesh of Christ that hid His divine glory—that glory which broke through on the mount of transfiguration, when Jesus' glory could not be contained within His flesh. That's what Peter was speaking about when he said, "[We] were eyewitnesses of His majesty . . . when we were with Him on the holy mountain" (2 Peter 1:16, 18b).

Second, notice the priestly imagery here. In Israel, the work of the high priest made it possible for the people to be cleansed and to approach the place of meeting in the tabernacle and later in the temple. But now we have a High Priest who goes not simply into the earthly tabernacle but who has entered into the heavenly tabernacle. He goes into the very presence of the Father on our behalf as our Mediator, as our High Priest. And because we have this—our own High Priest over the house of God—our consciences are cleansed.

Nobody wants to come near to God with an uneasy

conscience. Sin is one of the reasons why we like to keep a safe distance from Him. It goes back to the Garden of Eden. After that very first transgression, when God came into the garden, the last thing Adam and Eve wanted was to experience His nearness. Instead of rushing to Him, to greet Him and embrace Him as they had before, this time they ran for the woods. They wanted to avoid the nearness of God.

But here the New Testament tells us to come near with a firm faith, with full assurance, *because our consciences are clean.* We have had "our hearts sprinkled from an evil conscience and our bodies washed with pure water." Christ has taken the guilt of our sin and has covered us with the cloak of His righteousness, so that our sin is covered by His perfection. That's what makes it possible for us to come into the presence of God; otherwise, God wouldn't want to look at us. It is purely by God's grace that we can come into His presence at all.

PRACTICAL GUIDELINES

As Hebrews 10 continues, we find further instructions for worship. These include:

• *Assembling.* The author of Hebrews writes, "And let us consider one another in order to stir up love and good works, not forsaking the assembling of ourselves together, as is the manner of some. . . ." (vv. 24–25a). Surveys tell us that in the most vibrant churches in the United States on any given Sunday, at least 25 percent of the members are absent from worship services. Part of that is because of illnesses, vacations, travel, or other circumstances. But it also happens because people sometimes just don't feel like coming.

If we don't feel like going to church, we are to do it anyway. It's a privilege to come near to God and to worship with other believers, but it's also a sacred duty. I would be completely derelict in my duty if I didn't tell you that God takes worship attendance very seriously, just as this admonition shows. So if we get up and don't feel like going to church and want to go to the beach instead, we must say to ourselves: "Wait a minute, if I do this, I'm neglecting the God who has redeemed my soul from the pit. Therefore, I'm going to church."

• *Exhorting.* The passage goes on to say that far from neglecting to gather with other believers for worship, we should be "exhorting one another, and so much the more as you see the Day approaching" (v. 25b). "Exhorting" means encouraging. When we come to church on Sunday morning, we enjoy fellowship with one another. In the New Testament, fellowship was an important part of the Sunday experience of Christians. We benefit from the encouragement we get from being with friends who are also on a spiritual pilgrimage, people who know us, love us, and are praying for us. We, too, have the responsibility to encourage our fellow believers. Faithful attendance at worship is one way in which we can encourage one another.

GLORIFYING GOD

The principle that transcends the ages is that what we do on Sunday morning must add to the sense of the unsurpassed majesty of God. "And before all the people I must be glorified" (Lev. 10:3). In the Old Testament, the Hebrew word that is usually translated as "glory" is *kabod*. Its roots literally mean "that which is heavy" or "that which is weighty." *Kabod* refers to God's heaviness or weightiness—His transcendent and eternal dignity, which commands respect and homage from every creature. Because of this aspect of His person, no one should come into the presence of the God of glory in a flippant and cavalier manner. If we really understand who God is and that we're in His presence, we will be on our faces before Him, giving Him the honor and the praise that He deserves.

The primary reason to be in church is to worship the living God, and for this we must bring a sense of reverence and adoration for His transcendent majesty. There's nothing common about this. We walk through the door. We step across the threshold. We enter into His presence. We know that God is not restricted to the building, but we are aware that this is a sacred hour that God has set apart and declared to be a holy time of visitation between Himself and His people. So we leave worldly cares and concerns for a while and focus on God. We come to hear a word from God, and it is the pastor's responsibility to make sure what we hear from the pulpit *is* the Word of God, not pop psychology. The power is in the Word, for it is the truth. That's what we all desperately need to hear, and more than once a week. And so we come to hear and respond in a way that will honor God, in a way that will honor His majesty.

We're talking about the sovereign God of the universe, before whom the nations tremble. If we do not learn to honor Him now, we will certainly tremble before Him later. The lesson of Nadab and Abihu should drive us to serious and careful reflection about how we worship God.

Chapter 4

SERVICE

For years, my mother-in-law regaled our family with rich tales of her life on a Midwestern farm before automobiles, airplanes, indoor plumbing, and electricity. Her stories, spun with a beaming face and glistening eyes, mesmerized my grandchildren, because she seemed to tell of life on some other planet. It was a life that included sleigh rides behind the family horse, visits to the privy in the dead of night, and no television, radio, or computers.

But then her stories stopped and her words became

mostly incoherent. Her face grew pale and somber. The gleam left her eyes. Though she continued to live with us in our home and still sat with us at the table, she could not feed herself. Multiple mini-strokes and one major stroke had left her a mere shadow of her former self. She was still "Grandma," but her life had come to be managed by caregivers who attended to her twenty-four hours a day.

It was sad to watch her weaken daily. Yet it was a study in grace to watch the tender care she received from her two caregivers. Both of these women were absolutely delightful. They told me their Christian faith had impacted their work, because caregiving is a real ministry. Indeed, they ministered to my mother-in-law with incredible tenderness, concern for her feelings, and attention to detail. As I watched the two women, I realized I was watching a model of biblical service in action.

The five practices we are exploring in this book are all *means of grace*. A means of grace is a tool or instrument that God uses to strengthen and nurture us so that we grow in conformity to Christ. We don't always think about service as a means of grace, but we grow as we serve. The more we are able to serve in the kingdom of God, the more Christ-like we become. So it was with my mother-in-law's caregivers. I could see what it was doing for their Christian growth to be in a service ministry.

ESSENTIAL SERVICE

Service is not an optional aspect of the Christian life. All believers are called to be servants of God. It may not be *professional* or *paid* service, but each of us is to serve in some way.

One of the primary places in Scripture where we see this truth is in the Old Testament story of the Exodus. It begins with the people of Israel in servitude to a foreign master:

Now there arose a new king over Egypt, who did not know Joseph. And he said to his people, "Look, the people of the children of Israel are more and mightier than we; come, let us deal shrewdly with them, lest they multiply, and it happen, in the event of war, that they also join our enemies and fight against us, and so go up out of the land." Therefore they set taskmasters over them to afflict them with their burdens. And they built for Pharaoh supply cities, Pithom and Raamses. But the more they afflicted them, the more they multiplied and grew. And they were in dread of the children of Israel. So the Egyptians made the children of Israel serve with rigor. And they made their lives bitter with hard bondage—in mortar, in brick, and in all manner of service in the field. All their service in which they made them serve was with rigor. (Ex. 1:8–14)

As they labored under this terrible bondage, the Israelites cried out to God for release. God heard their cries, and He responded by appearing to Moses in the burning bush and calling him to go to Egypt, confront Pharaoh, and lead the people of Israel out of their bondage. Notice what God said:

And the Lord said: "I have surely seen the oppression of My people who are in Egypt, and have heard their cry because of their taskmasters, for I know their sorrows. So I have come down to deliver them out of the hand of the Egyptians, and to bring them up from that land to a good and large land, to a land flowing with milk and honey, to the place of the Canaanites and the Hittites and the Amorites and the Perizzites and the Hivites and the Jebusites. Now therefore, behold, the cry of the children of Israel has come to Me, and I have also seen the oppression with which the Egyptians oppress them. Come now, therefore, and I will send you to Pharaoh that you may bring My people, the children of Israel, out of Egypt."

But Moses said to God, "Who am I that I should go to Pharaoh, and that I should bring the children of Israel out of Egypt?"

So He said, "I will certainly be with you. And this shall be a sign to you that I have sent you: When you have brought the people out of Egypt, you shall serve God on this mountain." (Ex. 3:7–12)

This is a glorious story of redemption, but there is great irony here. We see what God redeemed His people *from*, but we must not miss what God redeemed them *to*. He called His people out of Egypt, out of slavery, not to become autonomous or to do whatever they please. He called them to *serve Him*. The Israelites were called *out of* service to Pharaoh and *into* service to God.

In a very real sense, the Exodus of the Israelites from Egypt functions as an image to prepare us for the ultimate exodus that is accomplished through our Deliverer, Jesus. Christ came not to take us out of Egypt but to free us from bondage to Satan. Yet, when Christ delivers us out of this bondage, we, too, experience an exchange of masters. He calls us to be *His* servants.

Paul's favorite description of himself was *doulos*, which means "slave"—one purchased for service. He said the same status applies to all believers, for we all have been "bought at a price" (1 Cor. 6:20). We belong to the one who has paid for us in order to redeem us, and now we are called to serve Him.

We also see the idea of service in the moving story of what took place in Shechem toward the end of Joshua's life. He assembled the people to renew their oath to the covenant they had made with God. At that time, Joshua said to the people, "Now therefore, fear the LORD, serve Him in sincerity and in truth, and put away the gods, which your fathers served on the other side of the River and in Egypt. Serve the LORD!" (Josh. 24:14). He gave the people this mandate: "You've been serving the wrong things—the Canaanite deities, the pagan idols. Put those away and serve the Lord in sincerity and in truth."

Does that strike a chord? Remember Jesus' teaching to the woman of Sychar (John 4), which we examined at Chapter 3? Jesus told the Samaritan woman that God is seeking those who will worship Him in spirit and in truth. What Jesus said to the Samaritan woman is very similar to what Joshua said to all of the assembled people: "Serve [the Lord] in sincerity and in truth."

Joshua then went on to say, "If it seems evil to you to serve the LORD, choose for yourselves this day whom you will serve, whether the gods which your fathers served that were on the other side of the River, or the gods of the Amorites, in whose land you dwell. But as for me and my house, we will serve the LORD" (Josh. 25:15). There is a sense in which we *have* to be servants. But whom will we serve? Jesus Himself said, "No one can serve two masters" (Matt. 6:24). We can serve the living God and Christ, but if that "seems evil," that is, if we don't want to do that, we can serve Satan or the interests of this world. The commitment and motto of every Christian should be, "As for me and as for my house, we're going to serve the Lord with single-minded devotion."

AN AVERSION TO SERVING

Service, however, is not high on the list of things we enjoy. In our culture, we struggle with the image and role of the servant. We think it's beneath our dignity to fulfill that role.

Many years ago, when I was in seminary, I had a revelation about my own feelings in regard to servitude. During one summer vacation, I got a job in the maintenance department of a large hospital in Pittsburgh. One of my jobs was to sweep around the outside of the building every morning, cleaning up the cigarette butts and other refuse left from the night before. I cleaned the parking lots and the streets in front of the hospital, as well as the parking lot of the dormitory for the nursing students.

Now you have to understand that when I was in high school, there was a clearly defined "pecking order" of graduates. At the top was the "elite" group, those students who went away to college, and the next rung on the ladder was occupied by the students who enrolled in nurses' training. Since I had graduated from college and was now in graduate school, I was in the academic *creme de la creme*. But during the summer, I was literally pushing a broom.

In the mornings, while I swept the parking lots, the student nurses exited their dorm and I greeted them. My epiphany came when they tilted their caps up in the air and walked past me as though I were invisible. It was beneath their dignity to talk to me because I was a lowly servant, someone whose job it was to sweep the parking lot.

I'll never forget that experience. I wanted to say, "Wait! You don't understand. I'm a college graduate. You are just in nurses' school. You don't understand the pecking order here." I didn't like being treated like a servant. I remember wrestling with that afterward and thinking, "You're supposed to be a Christian, and here you were upset because someone regarded you as a servant." I knew that as a believer I was commanded to be a servant, but I didn't like being treated like one.

Jesus' disciples also struggled with servanthood. Matthew writes:

Then the mother of Zebedee's sons came to Him with her sons, kneeling down and asking something from Him. And He said to her, "What do you wish?" She said to Him, "Grant that these two sons of mine may sit, one on Your right hand and the other on the left, in Your kingdom." But Jesus answered and said, "You do not know what you ask. Are you able to drink the cup that I am about to drink, and be baptized with the baptism that I am baptized with?" They said to Him, "We are able." So He said to them, "You will indeed drink My cup, and be baptized with the baptism that I am baptized with; but to sit on My right hand and on My left is not Mine to give, but it is for those for whom it is prepared by My Father." (Matt. 20:20–23)

James and John confidently affirmed, "We can drink that cup that the Father has put before you." It was as if Jesus looked them over and replied, "You think so? You're prepared to take the cup of God's wrath? You're prepared to have all of God's people's sins imputed to you and to expose yourself to the full measure of God's judgment and justice on the cross? You think you can take that cup? I have to face a baptism of fire by which I will experience the fullness of hell. Can you handle that?" And they so calmly replied, "Yes, we can." In truth, they did not have a clue what they were asking of Jesus.

Now when the other ten disciples heard that James and John had made this self-aggrandizing request, they were greatly displeased with the two brothers. But Jesus quickly corrected them all. Matthew goes on to say:

> But Jesus called them to Himself and said, "You know that the rulers of the Gentiles lord it over them, and those who are great exercise authority over them. Yet it shall not be so among you; but whoever desires to become great among you, let him be your servant. And whoever desires to be first among you, let him be your slave—just as the Son of Man did not come to be served, but to serve, and to give His life a ransom for many." (Matt. 20:25–28)

Here Jesus gave a definition of greatness. He said to His disciples, "Whoever desires to become great among you, let him be your servant." This mandate was not given just to twelve people. It was for the whole kingdom of God. It is the law of the King that we are to imitate Him by being servants.

VARIED ROLES

Jesus placed a particular burden on the apostles that cost them their lives. He commanded them to go into the world and preach the gospel. That was their mission—to go to the Jew first, then to the Gentile. Yet for the church to fulfill this preaching mission, a host of menial tasks had to be cared for—such as the serving of tables:

> Now in those days, when the number of the disciples was multiplying, there arose a complaint against the Hebrews by the Hellenists, because their widows were neglected in the daily distribution. Then the twelve summoned the multitude of the disciples and said, "It is not desirable that we should leave the word of God and serve tables. Therefore, brethren, seek out from among you seven men of good reputation, full of the Holy Spirit and wisdom, whom we may appoint over this business; but we will give ourselves continually to prayer and to the ministry of the word."

And the saying pleased the whole multitude. (Acts 6:1–5a)

Every believer is called to ministry. We're called to see that all of the tasks of the kingdom take place—that the poor are ministered to, the gospel is proclaimed, the Word of God is taught, and worship takes place. But that doesn't mean that everyone is called to be an evangelist, a preacher, or a teacher. The New Testament tells us that God gives every Christian a gift to be used for the service of Christ. If your gift is teaching, then you had better teach; if it's preaching, you should preach; if it's evangelism, you had better evangelize. If your role is to be a caregiver to shut-ins, then be a caregiver to shut-ins. But each one of us is called to do our part, thus ensuring that all the ministry is fulfilled.

UNPROFITABLE SERVANTS

Luke 17 records the disciples coming to Jesus and asking Him for a raise. Not a raise in pay, however; what they wanted elevated was their faith. They obviously saw a link between their Lord's faith and His power. Note how Jesus responded to their request:

> And the apostles said to the Lord, "Increase our faith."
>
> So the Lord said, "If you have faith as a mustard seed, you can say to this mulberry tree, 'Be pulled up by the roots and be planted in the sea,' and it would obey you. And which of you, having a servant plowing or tending sheep, will say to him when he has come in from the field, 'Come at once and sit down to eat'? But will he not rather say to him, 'Prepare something for my supper, and gird yourself and serve me till I have eaten and drunk, and afterward you will eat and drink'? Does he thank that servant because he did the things that were commanded him? I think not. So likewise you, when you have done all those things which you are commanded, say, 'We are unprofitable servants. We have done what was our duty to do.'"
> (Luke 17:5–10)

What an odd way for Jesus to answer their request. He told them a story about servants coming in after completing their tasks in the field. He asked, "Does the master of the servants say, 'You've done such a great job—sit down, eat, drink, enjoy yourselves'? Or does he say, 'Now it's time for you to fix my meal. You set the table. You serve me. When all your tasks are done, then you can eat and drink'?" Jesus was teaching the apostles about servanthood.

Perhaps the single most important truth we can learn from this story is that we, who are God's servants, are *unprofitable* servants. When Jesus said that we are unprofitable servants, He did not mean that our service is of no value. Jesus frequently called His disciples to be productive. Rather, He meant that we gain no "bonus points" or merit from our service.

In the Middle Ages, a pernicious view sprang up that held that Christians not only can gain a certain kind of merit by the works that they perform, but they can even perform "works of supererogation"—works that are so meritorious, so valuable, that they are above and beyond what God requires from His people. The church taught that the excess merit from these works of supererogation was deposited in what was known as "the treasury of merit," and from there it could be distributed to people in purgatory who were lacking in merit. This idea was behind the whole controversy over indulgences in the sixteenth century, and it was a major point of dispute between Protestants and Roman Catholics. It all boiled down to the concept that it is possible for believers to perform works that are above and beyond the call of duty.

Jesus' words here in Luke 17 surely put this idea in its proper place. What deed could I possibly do that was not something God required of me in the first place? Remember, He commands us to be perfect, and we can't improve on perfection. We can't even hope to reach that goal. I have no "profit" of my own because I earn nothing by doing what I am required to do. That's why our redemption is by *grace* and grace *alone*. There is only one thing that I can place before God that is, properly speaking, my own—my sin. The only thing that can redeem me is not *my* work, but the work that *Christ has performed on my behalf*. He freely came to do the Father's will and to submit Himself to the law for our sake. He, and He alone, is a profitable servant.

If we serve out of an effort to earn our way into the kingdom of God, we're deceiving ourselves. The motivation for Christian service is love for God. We serve not to *earn* salvation, but *because* Christ already has purchased salvation for us. That truth lies behind the verse in Augustus Toplady's great hymn, "Rock of Ages," that says, "Nothing in my hand I bring, simply to thy cross I cling." Toplady understood that after we have done our best deeds, we remain unprofitable servants. No matter how exemplary our service, we gain nothing by it that we can offer to God to procure His favor.

My friend John Piper has awakened people to a concept of vital importance to our Christian faith—the *joy* to be found in rendering obedience to God. John stresses that the motive for our obedience should *not* be simply an abstract sense of duty. Of course, we sometimes do have to obey out of duty, and that is better than disobedience. There are times when we don't enjoy the prospect of obedience, but we can't just wait until we feel like doing it. But John is absolutely right: it should be our delight to obey God. We should be motivated to serve Him out of joy for what He has done for us, not out of grim obligation or as a means to gain heaven.

So we are "unprofitable servants"—at least in this world. But notice that the master in Jesus' parable told his servant, "afterward you will eat and drink." In this simple statement we find a hint of an idea that Jesus makes explicit in Matthew 16:27—in the next world, Christ will "reward each according to his works." We must be careful with that phrase "according to." It does not mean that our works *earn* a reward. But God in His grace will distribute rewards according to our service—even though our works don't deserve it. This is a gracious distribution of rewards; Augustine called it "God crowning His own gifts." So even when we receive the rewards of heaven, we receive them as people who, in and of ourselves, are unprofitable servants.

PRODUCTIVE SERVANTS

In Luke 19:12–27 Jesus gives us more important teaching about servanthood:

> Therefore He said: "A certain nobleman went into a far country to receive for himself a kingdom and to return. So he called ten of his servants, delivered to them ten minas, and said to them, 'Do business till I come.' But his citizens hated him, and sent a delegation after him, saying, 'We will not have this man to reign over us.'

"And so it was that when he returned, having received the kingdom, he then commanded these servants, to whom he had given the money, to be called to him, that he might know how much every man had gained by trading. Then came the first, saying, 'Master, your mina has earned ten minas.' And he said to him, 'Well done, good servant; because you were faithful in a very little, have authority over ten cities.' And the second came, saying, 'Master, your mina has earned five minas.' Likewise he said to him, 'You also be over five cities.'

"Then another came, saying, 'Master, here is your mina, which I have kept put away in a handkerchief. For I feared you, because you are an austere man. You collect what you did not deposit, and reap what you did not sow.' And he said to him, 'Out of your own mouth I will judge you, you wicked servant. You knew that I was an austere man, collecting what I did not deposit and reaping what I did not sow. Why then did you not put my money in the bank, that at my coming I might have collected it with interest?'

"And he said to those who stood by, 'Take the mina from him, and give it to him who has ten minas.' (But they said to him, 'Master, he has ten minas.') 'For I say to you, that to everyone who has will be given; and from him who does not have, even what he has will be taken away from him. But bring here those enemies of mine, who did not want me to reign over them, and slay them before me.'"

This is a parable of capitalism, a parable of productivity. Jesus was calling His people to delay their gratification. He wants us to invest in the future so that our investments may grow. Like the rich master who had to go away, Jesus has ascended into heaven and left us behind with certain treasures during His absence. What is His expectation? "When I come back, I expect to find that those things I have given you have gained in value, that progress has been made because My people have been productive servants." We may be "unprofitable," but that doesn't mean we're to be *unproductive*. We cannot say to ourselves, "Let's sleep in tomorrow or hide our gifts, so that when He comes back, we can say, 'Here are the gifts You gave us. Nothing happened to them. They're just as good as when You left.'" Jesus will not accept that. He will say, "I'll take that away from you and give it to the man who multiplied his gifts ten times, the one who used the gifts I gave him for the sake of the kingdom."

This is a heavy parable of service. It reveals that one of the worst things we can do is to waste the gifts that God has given us. Those gifts are given to us for Christ's sake, for His glory and honor. He's the one before whom all the inhabitants of heaven cast down their golden crowns beside the glassy sea (Rev. 4:6ff). They take their gifts and present them to Christ because they are His in the first place. And that is what we are to do with our service. We are to be productive servants.

FAITHFUL SERVANTS

The apostle Paul amplified our responsibilities. He noted, "Let a man so consider us, as servants of Christ and stewards of the mysteries of God. Moreover it is required in stewards that one be found faithful" (1 Cor. 4:1–2).

A steward in the ancient world was someone who was given the responsibility to manage a household. That person was entrusted with the possessions of the owner.

The chief requirement of the steward was faithfulness. An unfaithful steward was a crook, somebody who would steal from the owner. Paul was saying, "Do you realize that we apostles are servants, stewards of the mysteries of God? God has entrusted these things to us."

He went on to say:

> But with me it is a very small thing that I should be judged by you or by a human court. In fact, I do not even judge myself. For I know of nothing against myself, yet I am not justified by this; but He who judges me is the Lord. Therefore judge nothing before the time, until the Lord comes, who will both bring to light the hidden things of darkness and reveal the counsels of the hearts. Then each one's praise will come from God. (1 Cor. 4:3–5)

"My stewardship, my service," Paul said, "is not to be judged by men. The value of my stewardship will be judged by Christ and not by human beings—not by you and not even by myself, because I can't give an accurate assessment of my own service and obedience." None of us can read anyone else's heart. Only the searcher of human hearts can do that. That's why the service that we are to give is to be unto the Lord and before His scrutiny.

Paul gave one final instruction that all servants of the Lord must hear. In Ephesians 5–6, Paul gave exhortations to wives, to husbands, to children, to fathers, and, finally, to bondservants and masters. The message he gave to the bondservants applies to every servant of Christ: "Bondservants, be obedient to those who are your masters according to the flesh, with fear and trembling, in sincerity of heart, as to Christ" (Eph. 6:5). He was telling slaves to serve their owners as if they were serving Christ, a familiar idea among evangelicals, who believe all service is ultimately rendered to God. But please heed Paul's follow-up words: "not with eyeservice as men-pleasers but as bondservants of Christ, doing the will of God from the heart" (Eph. 6:6).

I would say that the greatest weakness in the church today is that many pastors keep looking over their shoulders for the approval of men. But as soon as pastors become slaves to human opinion, trying to please human beings instead of God, the message of Christ is compromised. No man-pleaser preaches the whole counsel of God.

Our servanthood should require no supervision. We should not need to have someone constantly watching us to insure that we are working. Our goal should be to please *Christ,* not perform merely for the applause of people. People-pleasers cannot be true servants of Christ. We must keep our eyes on Christ and not on the judges of this world.

On Sept. 11, 2001, we saw many models of selfless service in the actions of the firefighters, police officers, and rescue workers dealing with the attack on the World Trade Center in Manhattan. The firefighters who lost their lives rushing to rescue those trapped in the towers certainly were not people-pleasers. Their service was authentic.

This is the kind of service the followers of Christ should be seeking to render. This is what we are to do as disciples. Service is a sacred call to every Christian.

Chapter 5

STEWARDSHIP

It was 1947 and I was thrilled, for I was about to see my first major league baseball game. My uncle held my hand as we walked up the ramp toward our seats at Forbes Field. From our vantage point, I could see players warming up on the grass. I could see the ivy-covered walls, the old iron gate behind the monument in center field, and the high screen guarding the right-field stands where Babe Ruth hit his last home run.

Suddenly my uncle stopped. He said to me, "Hold onto your wallet!" I immediately did so. When we took our seats, I asked, "Can I let go of my wallet now?" My uncle said, "Yes." When I asked him why he had told me to do that, he said, "See that man over there with the turned-around collar? He's a priest. You always have to hold onto your wallet when a priest or a minister comes near. They're all out to get your money."

Thus, my first baseball game (Pirates 5, Reds 2) was also my first exposure to a cynical attitude toward tithing and charitable giving.

My father did not share my uncle's cynicism. He preached tithing to us as children. Every week I was required to put 10 percent of my allowance in the offering plate at church. I was introduced to this practice long before I was a Christian.

There is widespread cynicism today about giving to the church. Some unscrupulous televangelists and pastors have made it seem unwise, thanks to their lavish lifestyles. Yet the Bible clearly commands Christians to give and to practice good stewardship.

We take an offering every Sunday in our church. Right before the offering, I usually say, "Let us now worship God with our tithes and offerings." The point I'm stressing to our congregation is that giving should be an act of worship.

Stewardship is the last of the five means of grace we will consider in this book. Like Bible study, prayer, worship, and service, practicing good stewardship helps us grow in the likeness of the Lord Jesus Christ.

SACRIFICE AND STEWARDSHIP

The Bible's first recorded offering was brought by the brothers Cain and Abel. The book of Genesis tells us:

> And in the process of time it came to pass that Cain brought an offering of the fruit of the ground to the LORD. Abel also brought of the firstborn of his flock and of their fat. And the LORD respected Abel and his offering, but He did not respect Cain and his offering. And Cain was very angry, and his countenance fell. (Gen. 4:3–5)

Why was Abel's offering more pleasing than Cain's? Some think it was because Abel's offering was an animal—a blood sacrifice—while Cain's was merely fruit of the ground. Yet throughout the Old Testament, God made provisions for sacrifices such as Cain's; they were fully acceptable to Him. Cain offered this kind of sacrifice because he was a tiller of the ground, while Abel was a shepherd. The text doesn't indicate that being a shepherd was somehow holier than being a farmer.

Hebrews 11:4 provides the key: "By faith Abel offered to God a more excellent sacrifice than Cain, through which he obtained witness that he was righteous, God testifying of his gifts; and through it he being dead still speaks."

It seems that what pleased God was the manner in which Abel gave his offering: he gave it *in faith*. Presumably, Cain did not. Indeed, his faithlessness was soon manifested in his jealous rage against his brother.

We remember from our earlier look at worship that God seeks those who will worship Him in spirit and truth. Abel did that. He offered to God the sacrifice of praise by making his offering in faith. This is the essence of worship.

The idea of sacrifice goes to the heart of biblical faith. Foreshadowing the perfect redemptive work of Christ, Old Testament worship focused on the sacrificial system. When someone entered the Old Testament tabernacle, the first article of furniture he saw was the altar of burnt offering.

Christian churches today feature no altars. The days

of bloody sacrifices of animals are over. The perfect, once-for-all sacrifice of Christ has taken away that need:

For Christ has not entered the holy places made with hands, which are copies of the true, but into heaven itself, now to appear in the presence of God for us; not that He should offer Himself often, as the high priest enters the Most Holy Place every year with blood of another—He then would have had to suffer often since the foundation of the world; but now, once at the end of the ages, He has appeared to put away sin by the sacrifice of Himself. And as it is appointed for men to die once, but after this the judgment, so Christ was offered once to bear the sins of many. To those who eagerly wait for Him He will appear a second time, apart from sin, for salvation.

For the law, having a shadow of the good things to come, and not the very image of the things, can never with these same sacrifices, which they offer continually year by year, make those who approach perfect. For then would they not have ceased to be offered? For the worshipers, once purified, would have had no more consciousness of sins. But in those sacrifices there is a reminder of sins every year. (Heb. 9:24–10:3)

So the atonement of Jesus as our Great High Priest ended the Old Testament sacrificial system. However, it did not destroy the principle of sacrifice in the Christian life. We are still called to worship God and to give offerings to Him in that worship. Paul wrote in Romans:

I beseech you therefore, brethren, by the mercies of God, that you present your bodies a living sacrifice, holy, acceptable to God, which is your reasonable service. And do not be conformed to this world, but be transformed by the renewing of your mind, that you may prove what is that good and acceptable and perfect will of God. (Rom. 12:1–2)

We are to give ourselves to God as *living sacrifices*. This means we are to give our time, our energy, and our very selves to Him as acts of worship and gratitude. But we must always be aware that God has given us these and all things. Biblical giving, therefore, is done in the context of stewardship, our management of the good things the Father showers upon us.

The concept of stewardship begins with creation. Creation is celebrated not only in Genesis but throughout Scripture, especially in the Psalms, where God's ownership of the universe is declared: "The earth is the LORD's, and all its fullness, the world and those who dwell therein" (Ps. 24:1). God is the author of all things, the Creator of all things, and the owner of all things. Whatever God makes, He owns. What *we* own, we own as *stewards* who have been given gifts from God Himself. God has the ultimate ownership of all of our "possessions." He has loaned these things to us and expects us to manage them in a way that will honor and glorify Him.

The word that is translated "stewardship" in the Bible is the Greek word *oikonomia*, from which we get our word *economy*. It is two distinct words joined together to create a new word: *oikos*, which comes from the Greek word for *house*, and *nomos*, the Greek word for *law*. The word that is translated "stewardship" literally means "house law" or "house rule."

In the ancient culture, the steward was not the owner of the house. Rather, he was hired by the owner to manage his house affairs. The steward managed the property and was responsible to allocate the resources of the home. It was his job to make sure that the cupboards were filled with food, the money was taken care of, the grounds were tended, and the house was kept in good repair.

Humankind's stewardship began in the Garden of Eden, where God gave Adam and Eve full dominion over the entire creation. Adam and Eve were not given *ownership* of the world; rather, they were given the responsibility of *managing* it. They were to insure that the garden was tilled and cultivated, and not abused or exploited, and that the goods God provided were neither spoiled nor wasted. So what we are talking about, fundamentally, when we discuss biblical stewardship is responsibility for managing or allocating resources that do not belong to us. They belong, ultimately, to God.

I serve as president of Ligonier Ministries. With that job comes the responsibility that every top executive bears—the allocation of resources. We look at our ministry. We have a building to take care of; constituents to serve; personnel, computers, office equipment, and supplies to manage; a certain amount of money; and a certain amount of time in which to operate our ministry. We cannot be effective if we waste our people, our money, or our time, or if we mismanage our facility and equipment. To do any of that would be bad stewardship. We understand that handling our resources takes wisdom. If we spend them on one thing, we cannot spend them on something else.

Everyone, even a billionaire, functions with limited resources. In our households, we learn that if we spend $50 on clothes, that's $50 we no longer have for anything else. Every time we use a resource, we make a decision, and that decision reveals what kind of stewards we are. That's where God holds us accountable. God was interested in how Adam and Eve cared for the garden, and He is interested in how we take care of our ministries, personal lives, homes—every aspect of life. All of these areas require managing and allocating resources.

One of the most gripping stories in the New Testament is Jesus' parable of the prodigal son. This young man received an inheritance he did not earn—his father just gave it to him. But as soon as he received it, instead of trying to increase his new-found wealth or investing it (as we saw in the parable of the servants in Chapter 4), he went far from home and wasted it on wine, women, and song. He ended up living in a pigsty.

This young man is known as a "prodigal" because he wasted his father's resources. Worse, he was wasting his life, the greatest failure of stewardship. Each one of us has been placed on this planet by God to glorify, honor, and serve Him with what we produce and how we live. A wasted life is a tragedy. That was the story of the prodigal son—until he came to his senses. He finally went back to his father's house in repentance, willing to give up his rights as a son and to be treated as a hired servant. Instead, his father welcomed him home and held a great celebration for his return—a beautiful picture of the grace and mercy of God for prodigals of all kinds.

THE TITHE IN THE OLD TESTAMENT

At the center of the biblical concept of stewardship is the tithe. We see it instituted as law in the Old Testament, where God declared, "All the tithe of the land, whether of the seed of the land or of the fruit of the tree, is the LORD's. It is holy to the LORD" (Lev. 27:30).

The tithe is one of the simplest, wisest, and most beautiful laws God ever gave His people because it was so manifestly fair. The word *tithe* means "tenth." The basic principle was that every person was to return one tenth of his increase to the Lord on an annual basis. This meant that everybody gave the same *percentage* but not the same *amount*. If a man raised livestock and ten calves were born to him during the year, he was required to return one calf to God. If he had a hundred calves, he would have to give ten. The same principle applied for those who grew wheat. If a farmer's yield was one hundred bushels of wheat, he had to give ten bushels to God. In modern terms, a person who made $10,000 in a year would return $1,000 in tithe. A person who earned $1 million per year would return $100,000. The rich person returns far more money, but gives the same percentage as the poor person.

Under this system, there was no way for politicians to use economics to gain political power, as sometimes happens today. The leaders could not say, "Some of you are going to pay nothing, but some of you are going to pay five percent, some of you are going to pay fifteen percent, and some of you are going to pay forty percent." That creates hostility and envy. In a sense, the tithe was the original flat tax. A poor man might pay nothing more than the widow's mite, while a wealthy man might have to pay a hundred thousand pieces of gold. The amounts were very different, but the set percentage made it fair.

Trouble developed in the Old Testament when the people held back on paying their tithes. In doing so, they were not obedient to God's law. We read in Malachi:

"Will a man rob God?
Yet you have robbed Me!
But you say,
'In what way have we robbed You?'
In tithes and offerings.
You are cursed with a curse,
For you have robbed Me,
Even this whole nation.
Bring all the tithes into the storehouse,
That there may be food in My house.
And try Me now in this,"
Says the LORD of hosts,
"If I will not open for you the windows of
    heaven
And pour out for you such blessing
That there will not be room enough to receive it."
(Mal. 3:8–10)

This was not the local minister giving an appeal for funds. This was God speaking to His covenant people. He asked a very pointed question: "Would you steal from God Himself?" The people naturally shrank back in horror at such a question. They replied, "Of course we would never rob You!" But God said: "You *have* robbed me. You have done it by keeping back for yourself that which belongs to Me and that which I have required of you—the tithe."

In response, God challenged the people, saying, "Why don't you test Me and see what I will do? If you honor Me, if you obey Me, I'm going to open up the windows of heaven and pour out so much blessing upon you that you're not going to have room to put it." God challenged the Israelites to be faithful, promising that He would open the windows of heaven and pour out blessings upon them.

THE TITHE IN THE NEW TESTAMENT

Some people say that the tithe does not apply to the New Testament. I think it does. We see people continuing to tithe in the New Testament community in one of the earliest non-biblical books. The *Didache*—the so-called "Teaching of the Apostles," written either at the end of

the first century or early in the second—includes a significant portion that addresses the question of supporting the
work of the kingdom. The tithe principle is clearly communicated there. Thus, we see that the primitive Christian community continued the practice of tithing.

It seems, however, that very few Christians believe the
tithe still applies. A poll of people claiming to be evangelical Christians indicated that only 4 percent of them
tithe. A similar poll indicated that the average percentage
of income evangelical Christians give to God's work is less
than 2.5 percent. If the tithe principle is still in effect and
the polls are accurate, then 96 percent of professing evangelical Christians are systematically robbing God.

This paltry giving affects the church in very negative
ways. To understand the repercussions of our failure to
tithe, we must remember why God instituted the tithe in
the first place. He had separated one of the twelve tribes of
Israel, the tribe of Levi, for ministry. The Levites were set
apart to take care of the spiritual and educational responsibilities of the nation, and the tithe was designated for
their support. Thus, the people's failure to bring the tithe
hurt the Levites' livelihood.

In establishing this structure, God demonstrated that

He understood market economics, wherein the marketplace establishes the "value" of goods and services. He knew that, left to themselves, people value doctors, business entrepreneurs, and even entertainers more highly than ministers or educators. Knowing this human tendency, God said, "I am instituting the tithe to make sure that these people who are doing these things on which I put a supreme value will receive a proper payment."

The same tendency is manifest in the United States today, where the two lowest-paid groups are pastors and teachers. This can only mean that we place a lower value on the work they perform in our midst than that of other professional groups. I have actually heard leaders of church boards say they keep their pastors' salaries low in order to keep them humble and reliant upon God. They want to insure that ministers are truly dedicated to their work and are willing to sacrifice to carry it out.

However, a minister who is being underpaid can hardly help but conclude that people do not appreciate his work. Because I work with so many pastors, I know that many of them experience a profound sense of discouragement because they feel that people do not appreciate their labor. I don't know of any men who went into the ministry to get rich, but most of them want to support their families, and an inability to do that is a constant concern and burden. We need to remember that God tells us, "The laborer is worthy of his wages" (1 Tim. 5:18b).

Failure to tithe also limits the ministry of the church. One of the greatest barriers to expanding the kingdom of Christ in this world is financial. A fundamental principle is at work here. If we have $100 to work with in ministry, we are limited by that dollar amount. We can waste that money and do only $10 of actual work. But even if we are expert managers and scrupulous stewards, we cannot do $110 of ministry. Christian ministry depends upon Christian giving. That giving always and everywhere determines the extent of ministry.

WHAT IS THE STOREHOUSE?

That brings up a controversial question with respect to financing the kingdom: where should we give our tithes?

We saw that God commanded the Israelites, saying, "Bring all the tithes into the storehouse that there may be food in My house" (Mal. 3:10a). In the Old Testament, the tithe, either in animals or produce, was brought to a central location, the storehouse, which was managed by the Levites. The whole tithe from the whole nation was brought into this single receiving place, and then was distributed by the Levites according to the needs of the people.

Some Christians believe that means the church should have a single storehouse, a place to which all tithes go and from which they are then distributed. However, we must remember that the people of Israel had a central sanctuary. When the New Testament church began, churches were established in every town and every city—in Ephesus, in Corinth, in Thessalonica, and so on. No longer was there one central sanctuary. So the idea of bringing tithes into one central storehouse is problematic.

Other Christians believe that the local church is the storehouse, so it is the only appropriate place for us to give our tithes. But nothing in the New Testament equates the local church with the Old Testament storehouse. If we believe that the local church *is* the storehouse, we have to argue that all tithes should go to a central location for an entire denomination or even an entire nation. All tithes would have to go to a central receiving house, to be distributed from there. I have never heard of a local church that favored that kind of structure.

It is simply not biblical to require a person to give his

or her entire tithe to a local church. I do believe that the lion's share of it should go to the local church. But I am also mindful of a prudential warning to Christians in the *Didache*: "Let your donation sweat in your hand before you give it." That's an interesting metaphor. Notice that the injunction is not for your hand to squeeze the money so hard that you never give it. That's not the point. The point is to be very careful, very discerning about where you give your donation. But I also think this injunction implies liberty in the giving of the tithe. That means your giving may include a seminary, a Christian college, or other worthy ministries.

I often hear people say, "I'd like to tithe, but I can't afford to." I honestly believe that if you invest in the kingdom of God, you won't lose anything in the final analysis. Tithe from the top, and learn to do that as early as you can in life. Parents, if you give your child a $1 allowance, make sure that he or she puts the first 10 cents into the collection plate on Sunday, so your child learns the principle of the tithe early. Also, we ought to regard our giving to the Lord just as we think about our "giving" to the government. We know we cannot spend the tax the government takes out of our paychecks; we must live on our "take-home" pay. But our obligation to God takes precedence over our obligation to government. God should get paid first, "from the top." If you want to know how serious you are about investing in God's kingdom, look at your checkbook. It is an objective, concrete record of where your treasure is, and that tells you where your heart is.

THE BEST INVESTMENT

We live in a country that was built on the principle of capitalism, and the fundamental idea of capitalism is *delayed gratification*. Instead of taking the money we make and spending it all now, we save it and invest it. This allows our capital to go to work for us, expanding our wealth. While you are sleeping, as it were, your money is working for you. I think that's a very wise way to manage one's personal income. If you make $10 an hour, you should say to yourself, "OK, I'm going to live on $8 an hour. Then I'm going to take $1 and give it to God, and the other dollar I'm going to invest." The sad reality is that we don't want to do that. Rather, we spend $12 for every $10 that we make, which has become the American way. But delayed gratification means that you invest to increase.

The Bible teaches that we are to invest in the kingdom

of God, and I really believe that is the best investment we can ever make, because it has eternal returns. These returns are not just for us but also for our families, especially for our children and grandchildren. This generation of Christians must invest in the things of God for the sake of the next generation. In doing this, we follow Jesus' admonition: "Seek first the kingdom of God and His righteousness, and all these things shall be added to you" (Matt. 6:33).

Let me encourage you, when you are allocating your resources, to think about how you can invest in Christ's kingdom. That includes your time, your labor, your equipment, and your money. That's how we support the ministry of Christ. If you return to God what He asks of you, then you can enjoy the rest as long as you use it wisely.

In the final analysis, giving itself is a grace that God gives. It is one of the important steps to spiritual growth.

Bible reading, prayer, worship, service, and stewardship—these are five key disciplines for a productive Christian life. All five are vital to our spiritual health and the health of Christ's church. If we as Christians will apply ourselves faithfully to them, we will be able one day to say with Paul, "I have fought the good fight, I have finished the race, I have kept the faith" (2 Tim. 4:7).

Chapter 6

QUESTIONS AND ANSWERS

I n this final chapter, I would like to touch briefly on various other issues related to the means of grace and growth in the Christian life, using a question-and-answer format.

DOES GOD HEAR, ACT ON, OR GRANT THE PRAYERS OF UNBELIEVERS?

There are different ways to look at this issue. On the one hand, of course, God hears every prayer in the sense that

He is cognizant of them. On the other hand, the Bible tells us God hates the prayers of unbelievers (John 9:31; 1 Peter 3:12). The hypocrisy of an unbeliever's prayer is a stench in His nostrils, so there is a sense in which God refuses to hear such entreaties.

However, I do believe God may do things in response to the prayers of unbelievers out of sheer grace. One of the most moving moments of my life occurred when I was in high school, while I was still unconverted. My older sister was giving birth to her first child, and after she bore that child, she suffered life-threatening hemorrhaging. It was very serious. She was in critical condition and her life was hanging in the balance for several hours. During that time, I was left alone in the hospital. In my grief and terror, I went into the hospital chapel and prayed a "foxhole prayer"—the kind of prayer a soldier might pray, seeking deliverance from danger in combat. I prayed my heart out for the life of my sister. As I said, I was an unbeliever at that point, but I knew there was a God, so I cried out to him in that time of need. My sister's life was spared, and I counted that as a kind and generous divine response to my prayer.

SHOULD WORSHIP SERVICES HAVE ANY FOCUS ON UNBELIEVERS?

I think we should design Sunday morning worship for seekers—but when I use the word *seekers*, I am talking about Christians, because the New Testament tells us that the only people who seek after God are those who have been converted by the Holy Spirit. We have the idea that there are all kinds of unbelievers who are desperately seeking for God, but that God is fleeing from them and hiding. But the Bible makes it very clear that nobody in his natural state seeks after God. Seeking God is the business of the Christian. We don't start seeking after God until He finds us. Once we are converted, we embark on the lifelong quest to know God as deeply as we can. So Sunday morning worship should fill believers' minds and hearts with the Word of God.

IF WORSHIP SERVICES ARE PRIMARILY FOR BELIEVERS, IS THERE A PLACE IN THOSE SERVICES FOR AN INVITATION TO SALVATION IN CHRIST?

Sunday morning worship is not to be designed for the unbeliever but for the believer, because that time is the assembling together of God's people. Yet the Scriptures tell us that, as Augustine pointed out, the church is always a *corpus per mixtum*, a mixed body. Jesus said there will be tares among the wheat. So I always assume that there are people in worship services who are unconverted, who have never really come to Christ. For that reason, in my sermons I often direct my comments specifically to unconverted people, admonishing, warning, exhorting, and so on, calling them to faith in Jesus Christ. However, I never use the term *invitation* because I think it is utterly unbiblical. I don't see where God *invites* people to come to Christ. Rather, God *commands* people to come. When you get an invitation to an event, you usually can decline it with impunity. But you can't decline the call of the gospel with impunity. If you decline that call, you seal your eternal damnation.

The other thing that concerns me is that in the evangelical world, we have confused the making of professions with saving faith. Everyone who has saving faith is called to profess that faith. But we somehow have come to think that public profession itself gives people salvation. So we have myriad people who have a false sense of assurance because they can say, "I walked down the aisle," "I raised my hand," or "I said the sinner's prayer." Walking an aisle never justified anyone. Raising a hand never got anyone into the kingdom of God. Saying the sinner's prayer doesn't automatically change anyone's heart. The only way to be saved is through faith in Christ alone, and no preacher can manufacture that. But in our zeal to win people, we do anything we can to get people up and out of their chairs. Then we end up with "evangelistic statistics," which usually aren't very accurate or helpful.

HOW OFTEN SHOULD A CHURCH CELEBRATE THE LORD'S SUPPER?

I honestly don't know of a biblical answer to this question. John Calvin was convinced the Lord's Supper should be observed weekly, but the authorities of Geneva would not allow that. Churches today are all over the map. Some observe the sacrament weekly, while others have Communion only three or four times a year, and everything in between.

At my church, we wrestled with this issue for a long time, wondering whether we should have the Lord's Supper weekly. One of the concerns was that if we had it weekly, people would begin to take it for granted and would miss the significance of the event. On the other hand, we believe in the real presence of Christ in the Lord's Supper, not in a consubstantiational (the Lutheran view) or transubstantiational (the Roman Catholic view) way, but we embrace Calvin's view—that Christ really comes to meet with His people at the table in a special redemptive way. We believe the supper really is a sign and a seal, given for our edification. It's vital and rich to our spiritual growth. At present, we celebrate the supper monthly, but we continue to study and pray over this question.

SHOULD ELEMENTS OF THE LITURGICAL CHURCH CALENDAR— MAUNDY THURSDAY, LENT, EPIPHANY, AND SO FORTH— BE RECOGNIZED IN CORPORATE WORSHIP?

There have been different directions as far as the structure and form of worship in historic evangelicalism, and even in the Reformed tradition. The great issues in the British Reformation between the Church of England and the Puritans had to do with questions of this sort. Some ministers lost their positions or were even thrown in jail because they refused to follow the church calendar.

That stance was pioneered by the magisterial Reformers. Calvin's great passion was the reform of worship. He saw that the great error of the medieval church was the development of patterns of worship and liturgy that led to the eclipse of the gospel. He believed that the Roman Catholic Church, in its emphasis on images, had fallen into radical idolatry. So Calvin, and the Puritans who followed him, favored eliminating all such elements. He admitted there was no absolute, principial biblical prohibition against some of the things he wanted to remove, but for him, it was simply prudent to do away with them because the people had come to associate images and other liturgical elements with worship practices. He wanted to focus on the unadorned gospel. And so he radically simplified the worship service, and among those things he eliminated was use of the church calendar.

I think the Reformers overreacted at some points. For instance, I think they missed the sanctity of beauty that God established when He ordained patterns of worship in the Old Testament. The first people who were said to be filled with the Holy Spirit were those artisans and craftsmen whom God ordained to adorn His sanctuary. For that reason, I don't believe our sanctuaries need to be as simple and unadorned as the Reformers and Puritans dictated. Likewise, I think it is perfectly acceptable to follow the church calendar. In my church, we observe Maundy Thursday, Good Friday, Easter, and so on, and we use paraments that follow the church calendar.

JESUS CRITICIZED THE PHARISEES FOR THEIR LEGALISTIC ATTENTION TO TITHING. WAS HE SAYING THAT TITHING WAS WRONG?

Jesus certainly took the Pharisees to task for their hypocrisy. In Matthew 23, we find a long lists of woes that Jesus pronounced upon these religious leaders. In the midst of that monologue, He said, "Woe to you, scribes and Pharisees, hypocrites! For you pay tithe of mint and anise and cummin, and have neglected the weightier matters of the law: justice and mercy and faith. These you ought to have done without leaving the others undone" (v. 23). We must be careful as we analyze this verse. Jesus was not attacking the Pharisees for their attention to tithing. Rather, He was pointing out that they had failed to give the same attention to other matters that they gave to tithing. Nowhere in this verse does Jesus say they were wrong to tithe. In fact, He says they should be giving the same level of attention to what He called "weightier matters," such as justice, mercy, and faith, but *not at the expense of tithing*. They needed to do both, not abandon tithing to tackle more important things.

It is interesting that our Lord did not include tithing among the "weightier matters" of the law. That doesn't mean God won't be upset if we rob Him by failing to tithe. But it does imply that tithing is a small thing in the sense that it is one of the easiest things to do in the Christian life. It's so easy, even the hypocritical Pharisees could handle it. But we often find it to be one of the hardest disciplines to begin and maintain.